Architectural Guide
Sofia

Authors
Todor Boulev
Konstantin Boyadzhiev
Rossitsa Bratkova
Grigor Doytchinov
Hristo Ganchev
Teodora Kanalieva
Georgi Stanishev
Vassil Vakarinov
Aneta Vassileva

Text editor
Rossitsa Bratkova

Architectural Guide
Sofia

Edited by Georgi Stanishev

DOM
publishers

Street scene in downtown Sofia

Contents

How to use this guide
All projects are numbered and marked on the maps

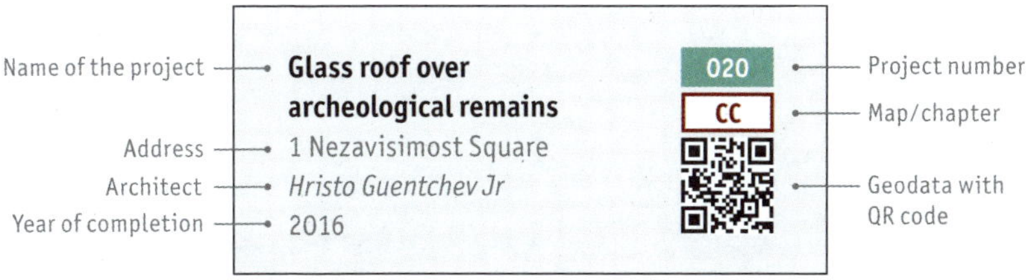

**Red Apple Apartments (166), 24 Byala Cherkva Street,
Architects: AEDES Studio/Plamen Bratkov, Rossitsa Bratkova (2012)**

Sofia in Time and Space

Todor Boulev, Grigor Doytchinov, Hristo Ganchev, Georgi Stanishev

Imagine a valley surrounded by the Balkan Mountains to the north and the Vitosha Mountain to the south. The time is Late Antiquity, when two important routes intersected at this point: one leading from Northern Europe to Thessaloniki; the other, from the West to the East, linking Singidinum (now Belgrade) to the Bosphorus, where the new Byzantine Empire was soon to rise. Near the crossroads lies a hot mineral-water spring, directly between two mountain rivers, Perlovska and Vladayska, enclosing the hill, now crowned by the St Alexander Nevski Memorial Cathedral. Next to the hospitable natural conditions of the place, the spring was the basic reason for the formation of the settlement and the road network. Some of the ancient roads leading to the spring still exist in the city today: the boulevards Dondukov to the east, Maria Luiza to the north, and Boris III to the south-west. Of a more local meaning are the historic traces of both Vitosha Boulevard and Graf Ignatiev Street, which link the city with Vitosha Mountain to the south. This is a general picture of the conditions that gave rise to the settlement of the valley between the 7th and 6th millenniums BCE and later to the formation of the ethno-cultural Thracian community during the Bronze Age. The hot mineral-water spring is still in Sofia today and its water flows from about 30 drinking fountains, which are freely accessible in the ancient heart of the city.

The Stabilising of Sofia's Urban Core during Antiquity and the Middle Ages

Between the 9th and the 7th centuries BCE the Thracian tribe of the Serds established their settlement, known as Serdonpolis, at the location of Sofia's current core. In the 1st century CE it was conquered by the Romans and renamed Serdica. A look at the plan of Sofia today reveals a clear mono-centrality, based on the Ancient Roman layout. Traces of Serdica can be found in the very centre of the city, starting from segments of the Roman fortification wall, exposed in some of the underground passages, up to the unique, well-preserved Roman rotunda (the current St George Church) within the Sheraton Hotel courtyard and the Roman amphitheatre inside the Arena di Serdica Hotel. The city preserved its characteristic features throughout the Byzantine periods (5th–9th, 11th–12th centuries), when the St Sofia Basilica was erected, as well as during the two Bulgarian empires

Figure 1 **Cadastral plan from 1887**

(10th and 12th–14th centuries). A real jewel of the latter period is the Boyana Church on the outskirts of Sofia, most famous for its proto-Renaissance wall paintings from the 14th–15th centuries. Official sources point to this period as the time the name 'Sofia' was first mentioned. In 1392 the city was conquered by the Ottomans. The transformation of the Roman orthogonal grid into the organic medieval pattern probably began in the 12th century and continued during the Ottoman period, but the bedrock set by the Romans has not changed over the centuries and remains the focal point of the city even today. Though there is not much left from the Medieval period in Sofia, some Ottoman mosques from the 16th–18th centuries can still be seen. Saved from destruction after the National Liberation in 1878, the Banya Bashi Mosque (16th century), located near the spring capture, is still a Muslim temple, and was probably designed by the famous Ottoman architect Mimar Sinan. Two other mosques have been converted – the Buyuk Mosque into an archaeological museum and the Kodzha Dervish Mehmed Pasha Mosque into the St Sedmochislenitsi (Saints Cyril and Methodius and their five disciples) Church. In the year of Liberation, Russian military engineers made the first cadastral map, which showed the structure of the city at that time. On a plan from 1887, Sofia seems to be a typical amorphous Ottoman settlement, which organically followed the topography and was composed of relatively autonomous units, called *mahalas* (see figure 1). The only public spaces were the marketplaces and the casual extensions at street crossings.

Urbanism and the Architecture of Modern Times

The pro-European political and cultural orientation that occurred after Liberation was a logical consequence of the Bulgarian National Revival, which began in the 18th century as a delayed transition from the Middle Ages to Modernity. The final phase of that revival was the establishment of public institutions and the governmental sovereignty, as well as the nomination and announcement of Sofia as the new capital in 1879. The Bulgarian educated elite stood for a complete rebuilding of the oriental image of the city. The lack of local experts led to the implementation of European urban-design models, introduced by foreign specialists, predominantly from Central Europe. The first regulation plan was elaborated by Licurgo Amadey, Vatzlav Roubal, and Georgi (Irji) Prošek in 1879, and defined the city's edges following the Ottoman defensive trenches. The planners kept and prolonged the traces of the ancient Cardo and Decumanus as well as the main antique grid. As a result of this adaptive attempt, the newly designed landmark central square, now crowned by the St Nedelya Church, was moved slightly southwards from the core of the Ottoman settlement and currently corresponds to the location of the Roman forum. The planned ring-boulevard was a recurring element in the nineteenth century. European urbanism and the compositional analogy to the Ringstrasse in Vienna are evident. But despite the similarities, there were clear differences between the two plans: unlike Vienna's Ringstrasse, Sofia's ring road was planned as an outer urban extension. The organic medieval quarters enclosed between the main historic routes and the ring road were turned into an orthogonal grid. The overall spatial and architectural transformations of Sofia were initiated immediately after Liberation and were all accomplished within the next four decades. During that process the defacing of the traces of the Ottoman Empire was an intentional act of power, demonstrating the country's Western-oriented outlook and demarcating it from the Orient.

National Romantic Architecture: 1890s–1920s

A 1897 cadastre map after the Austrian architect Wilhelm Bartel illustrates that at that time the essential specifications of the 1879 plan had already been realised. Both the ring road and the centre of Sofia had been completed, as had the orthogonal street grid. This cadastre helps show the speed of urban change. The same year a new regulation plan was elaborated, outlining a secondary, outer ring-road. Its realisation was the finishing touch of an urban phase that was very important for the future development of the city. The construction of the Central Railway Station in the north at the end of the 19th century was followed by a further expansion of the city (see figures 2a and 2b). In the lead up to the First World War, Sofia's urbanism was manifested in two principle phases. During the first one, foreign experts focused their activities upon the urban modernisation of the Ottoman settlement. The second phase took place in the time between the 1890s and the First World War. Besides spatial expansion, its main focus was the building of a new identity for the city, implemented by a number of European architects, such as the Austrians Friedrich Grünanger (Sofia Synagogue), Hermann Helmer, and Ferdinand Fellner (National Theatre); the Russians Alexander Pomerantsev (Saint Alexander Nevski Memorial Cathedral), Mihail Preobrazhenskiy (Saint Nikolay Russian Church); and more than 200 other architects from 15 European countries. A decade later the first generation of native Bulgarian architects, who had completed their education in European academies, further developed contemporary European tendencies in the architecture of Sofia. The most prominent among them were Nikola Lazarov, Georgi Fingov, Yordan Milanov, and Petko Momchilov. Thus, on the eve of the First World War, Sofia's architectural features were defined by some of the sporadic neohistorical styles that spread in Europe at the turn of the century, such

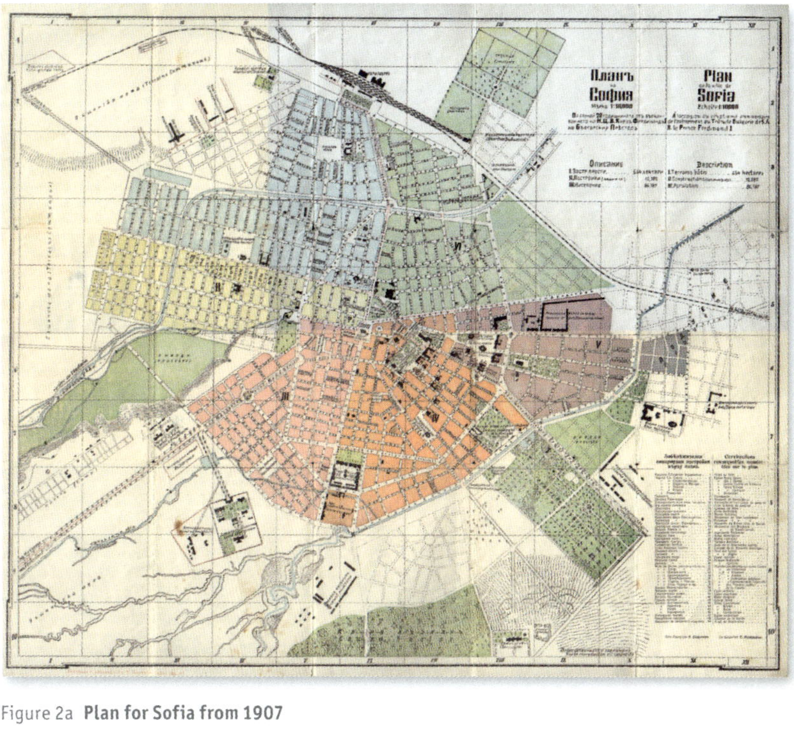

Regional Historical Museum Sofia

Figure 2a **Plan for Sofia from 1907**

Figure 2b **Sofia plan from 1907, on a topography from 1877–1878**

as neoclassical and neobaroque eclecticism, and the art nouveau of the Vienna Secession. The post-Liberation period was also related to the development of National Romanticism, a style based on medieval Byzantine building traditions and their interpretation in the First and Second Bulgarian empires. The radial-ring system was fully complete in the urban composition after the First World War. In a plan from 1919 the main features of European urban planning from the 19th century are clearly recognisable (see figure 3).

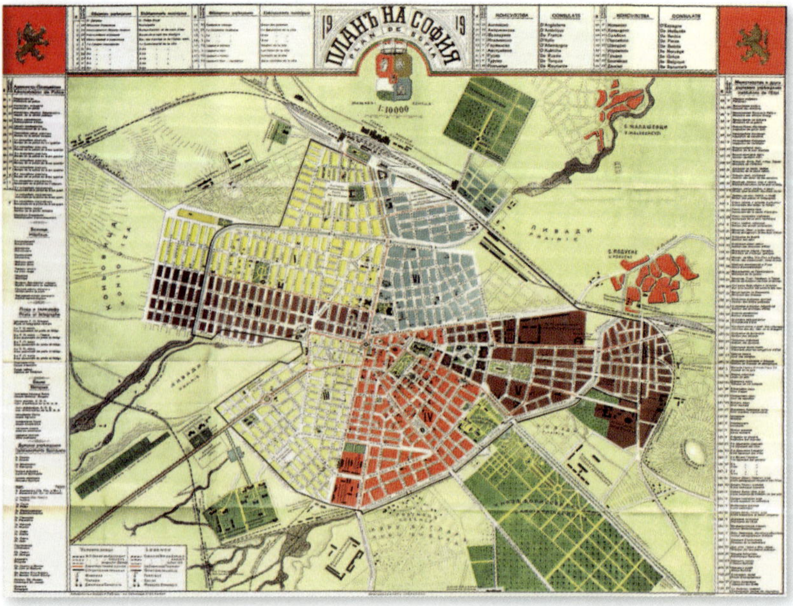

Figure 3 **Sofia plan from 1919**

All images: Regional Historical Museum Sofia

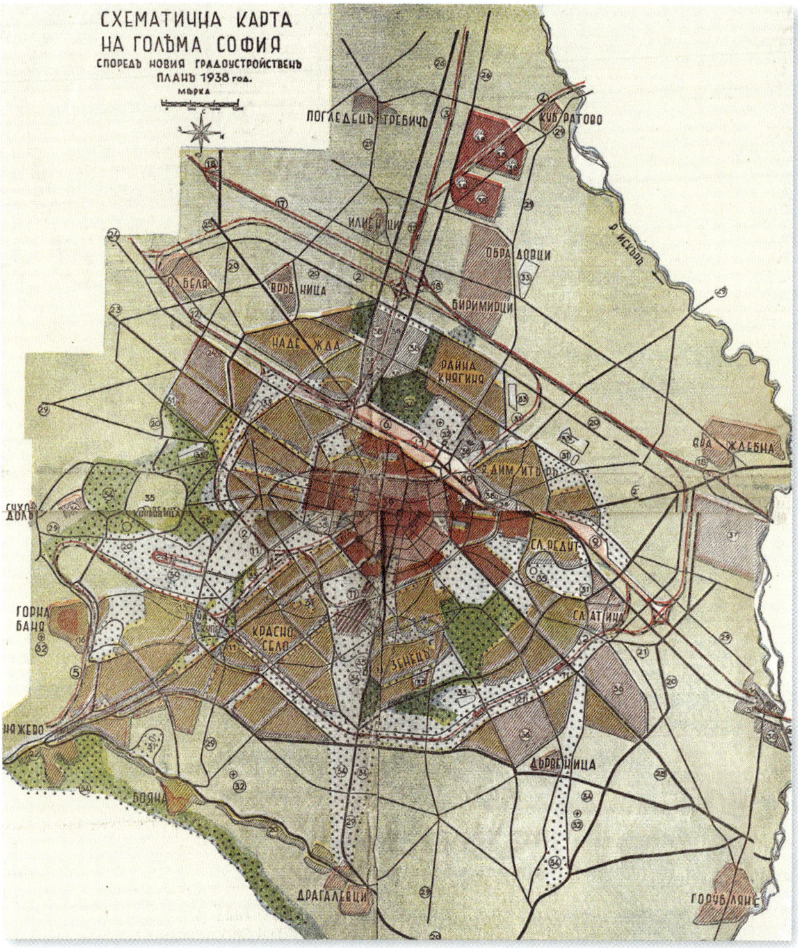

Figure 4 **Adolf Mussmann's land use plan for Sofia from 1938, on a topography from 1877–1878**

Modernist Urbanism and Architecture: 1920s–1940s

The systematic urban design of the post-Liberation period underwent a setback focused on Sofia's periphery: the city became surrounded by refugee quarters which sprang up on undeveloped territories, thus establishing the 'third suburban area' to the east, which is today a regular part of the city. This was the result of fast industrialisation and of the demographic crisis in the wake of the First World War, which was caused by unprecedented mass migration from Macedonia, Thrace, and the Morava region. During the interwar period the city's population increased from 100,000 to 350,000. The 1930s are generally characterised by swift development, an economic upturn, and a building boom. The planning of the contemporary city started in 1934, when the authorities entrusted the German architect Adolph Mussmann with the elaboration of a new land-use plan. Mussmann's plan was an attempt to solve the Bulgarian capital's problems, and it still functions today. It was also the first theoretical planning approach in the history of the country (see figure 4). Its main concept was based on the development of infrastructure and the public transport system. The modernist vision of green wedges reaching the city centre from the outskirts had a considerable impact upon the future spatial development of the city. In order to regulate and hinder the city's extensive growth, the Mussmann plan suggested the zoning of the city's territory. Its rational proposals and focus on social factors corresponded to the modernist planning ideas of the interwar period. In the 1930s

Figure 5 **Master plan for Sofia city centre from 1947**

and 1940s the language and ideology of the Modern Movement were introduced to the city, although they were adapted to fit the local Balkan temperament, which does not favour extreme cosmopolitanism. Nevertheless, architects educated in Germany, Austria, France, and Italy, such as Georgi Fingov, Ivan Vasilyov, Georgi Ovcharov, Hristo Berberov, and others, marked the period with a respectable number of buildings based on the rhetoric of early European modernism and expressionism. This process developed in two parallel trends, one of them attempting to revive National Romanticism, and the other tending towards monumental classicism influenced by fascist architecture in Germany and Italy. Hence, Sofia's architecture of the interwar period reflects the complexities and contradictions between the Modern movements on the one hand, and the reborn interest in classicist planning and design, on the other. Expressed in various formal languages, the interpretations of classicism went on until the middle of the 1950s. In that way, the practice of a whole generation of architects presented and integrated both artistic interpretations of modernism and various expressions of classicism during the period from the 1930s to the 1950s, though in two fundamentally different sociopolitical systems: capitalism and socialism. The historic core of Sofia was established as the trade and business heart of the city before the Second World War. Consequently, the city zoning followed a tendency towards social separation. The more expensive buildings of higher aesthetic value were situated in the eastern and southern hilly parts of the city. At the same time the Orthodox and the Catholic churches, the Central Synagogue, and the Banya Bashi Mosque formed a multi-religious centre around the mineral hot-water spring. It seems that the *genius loci* of the two zones, developed over one millennium, is a sustainable one.

Architecture for the Socialist Society: the Stalinist Period 1948–1950s

The destruction caused by Second World War air raids broke the continuity of the formation of the city. The force of urbanisation and the increased migration gave new power to the urban development of Sofia and to the restructuring of its core in the postwar period. The implementation of the eclectic style of the Stalinist era did not start until 1948. Numerous pre-war projects, such as the National Library and the Telephone and Telegraph Hall, were accomplished in that period, supporting continuity and the genetic link to modernism and the monumental classicist approach of the 1930s. A factor of decisive importance for the reorganising of the urban space was the destruction of a substantial amount of residential buildings – about 12,000 – during the war, which gave way to a rigorous reshaping of the city centre. The political aim was to establish a representative centre, demonstrating the demarcation from the bourgeois past and the orientation to the socialist future. Nevertheless, the city core preserved its spiritual, administrative, trade, and business functions. The master plan for the centre from 1947 introduced the Stalinist principles of urban design (see figure 5). The inherited structures were reorganised to establish the Largo ensemble of buildings as a representative axis, intended to underline the dominant position of Party House, the headquarters of the Communist Party, symmetrically flanked by the buildings of the Council of Ministers and the Central Universal Store to the north, and the Presidency and Balkan Hotel, to the south. The public square around St Nedelya Church and the one surrounding Banya Bashi Mosque, previously divided by a block, were unified into a large-scale open space, subordinated to the Largo. The unique Antique complex of the St George Rotunda and the small St Petka Samardzhiyska Church was carefully preserved, even though the conservation and exhibition of archaeological findings played a peripheral role in that period. After that, underground archaeological urbanism began and still continues today. The classicist approach of the Stalinist era led to a formal continuity in the development of public spaces in Sofia, linking the pre- and post-war fabric into one coherent tissue and thus forming traditional district blocks as the dominant urban pattern. The eclectic style followed the one practised in the Soviet Union and the other socialist countries, but also made use of some narrative ornaments of local traditions, fitting the formula of the socialist art expression 'national form, socialist content'. The construction of the buildings, which had started before the Second World War, continued and integrated well with the realities of the late 1940s and the 1950s, as in the cases of both the extensions of Sofia University, and the National Library.

The Revival of Modernist Values: 1960s–1970s

The dictate of socialist realism did not last long. The political changes in Bulgaria in 1956 and the following De-Stalinisation caused a prompt revival of the rationality of Modern architecture. The urbanism of the second half of the 1950s was focused on the intensive development of the city and the conversion of abandoned military territories into housing areas with public green spaces. The conversion and the intensification were both formulated as basic guidelines in the urban plan of 1961. The plan incited the development of the West and North parks, thus continuing the concept of laying out green wedges, such as Borisova Gradina, set at the turn of the century, and South Park, proposed in the Mussmann plan in 1934. The rational-utopian character of modernist urbanism, alongside fast-assembly building technologies, seemed to be the proper instruments for the rapid realisation of the new social aim: high-standard dwellings for citizens. From the 1970s onwards a substantial share of the new housing estates was concentrated over four clusters on the periphery of the city. The largest and most emblematic estates are Lyulin in the west and Mladost in the south-east, each accommodating more than 100,000 inhabitants. Besides the well-known criticisms of the mono-functionality and monotony of these residential clusters, the idea of building up territories on the periphery of the city had many positive aspects. Mainly it was an opportunity to protect the architectural heritage of the Bulgarian capital's historic core from the abstract patterns of modernism. However, ambitions for the total rebuilding of the urban core were nevertheless present in all the plans from the 1960s and 1970s. They did not fade until the end of the 1970s, under the impact of rapidly changing international practices. The declaration of almost 700 architectural monuments in Sofia strongly influenced planning and architectural design. Along with mass housing, the period was marked by the development of cooperative residential blocks, a specific Bulgarian model of private entrepreneurship. Following the rights of each family to buy or participate in the construction of a private apartment within a cooperative format, the proportion of private residence ownership in the whole country exceeded 80 percent. The cooperative format led to examples of good architectural quality and a human scale of the urban fabric in parts of the city dominated by privately or cooperatively owned residences. The 1960s and 1970s could be defined as the heroic period of the defence of modernist values, through the intensive development of hotels, offices, educational, sportive, and cultural buildings and complexes. The Bulgarian Telegraph Agency, Hotel Rila, Universiada Hall, the Festival Hall, Radio Sofia, the University of Architecture, Civil Engineering and Geodesy, and the House of Soviet Science and Culture are important milestones of the development of socialist modernity.

Reconstruction Projects of the 1980s

In 1980 the population of Sofia exceeded one million inhabitants. That increased the search for not only residential space in new districts and clusters, but also new locations for cultural, administrative, and business programmes in the growing capital. One particular urban programme that developed in that period was intended to strengthen the connection between the city centre and Vitosha Mountain through Lozenets Hill. It gave a clear preference to the south as a direction for the future extensions of the centre, and persisted as a guiding idea for the next decades. Initially located on the outskirts of the city, Lozenets Hill had already been surrounded by small-scale housing quarters in the 1930s. Although the conversion of the area had partially started in the 1950s and 1960s, its fast development began by the end of the 1970s, as a part of the preparation for the 1,300th anniversary of the Bulgarian State, celebrated in 1981. The jubilee was used by the government as a pretext to force the conversion of the linking zone into a new public centre, through the construction of the National Palace of Culture, with Alexander Barov as a principal architect, and the dominant Bulgaria Square in front of it. Gradually, the square, with its luxurious surroundings, turned into the main entertainment and recreational area of the city. It reoriented the city centre towards South Park and created a unique link between the urban core and the regional symbols – Vitosha Mountain and Lozenets Hill. In 1985 a logical intervention followed, and the central Vitosha Boulevard was turned into a pedestrian zone. The boulevard, which is the prolongation of the Ancient Roman Cardo Maximus, connects the Largo to Bulgaria Square and South Park. The forming of the pedestrian zones streamlined the planning of Sofia to the world tendencies of the time. The architecture of late socialism started to retreat from the doctrine of the modernist movement. Instead it became influenced by the postmodern trends in Europe and the orientation towards historical forms and a new monumentality. Modernist ideas in architecture were gradually exhausted by the end of the 1970s, defining a period of experimentation and the search for innovation. The use of internationally influential neobrutalist, metabolist, and then postmodernist rhetoric could be easily traced in the works of Nikola Nikolov, Georgi Berberov, Mihail Sokolovski, Ivan Tatarov, and other masters of the period. In that context it was not by accident that in 1984 Kisho Kurokawa received a commission to design a luxury hotel on Lozenets Hill, as a part of the New Otani chain. The stable economic and political situation in that period was a precondition for an 'official' type of architecture for public buildings, which ran parallel to the late modernist rhetoric with some classical overtones. Its appearance was generally defined by symmetrical compositions and imposing central spaces. Typical examples of that late modernism are the National History Museum, the Ministry of Foreign Affairs, and of course the National Palace of Culture. The international rise of postmodernism provoked some local reactions in the mid-1980s, in the form of a revival of National Romanticism, especially in the application of architectural ornaments and the so-called synthesis of the arts.

From the Hierarchical to the Spontaneous City

By the end of the 1980s Sofia's architecture and planning practices had encountered the professional disorientation and global chaos of the diffused value systems of postmodern times. The changing political and economic conditions meant Sofia's urbanism suffered from controversial and short-term vectors of interest, as well as from the conversion of the economic system into a market-based one. But soon the city development programmes returned to the urban interventions planned and developed since the end of the 1970s. Those were the westward extension of the city centre and the southward development axes, as well as the realisation of the metro system. The first important operations followed the model of the radial-ring urban system already established at the end of the 19th century. The redesign of the Vitosha Boulevard pedestrian zone turned it into the most frequented public space, meeting public approval. These realisations were followed by the reconstruction of the basic routes of the ring and radial roads. The transformations concerned the commercialisation and partial gentrification of the urban core, the suburbanisation on the periphery, and differentiation between urban areas. The inherited lack of proper commercial spaces, the poor utilisation of the inner city, and the inadequate privatisation and restitution of vast city territories led to many urban controversies and conflicts. These circumstances provoked a speedy intensification of the historical urban sectors and a remarkable over-densification of some of them. The dominant ensemble of political power from the socialist period started to lose its meaning in the urban silhouette. Thus, the changes in Sofia could be regarded as a process of balancing the urban structure. Some of the settlements in the suburban belt which have so far preserved their traditional rural character have become, in recent years, favourite places for the new bourgeoisie. The growing difference between the northern suburban territories and the southern areas at the foot of Vitosha split the city and turned its southern part into the most desirable residential area. The establishment of public models of governance and, since 2007, integration into the European Union have had a positive impact on the spatial organisation of the city, whose population today exceeds 1.3 million. The speedy realisation of underground public transport, the adaptation of the street network to current needs, the implementation of smart-city concepts, and the extension of the system of green areas all created fresh preconditions for the new urban and architectural image of Sofia. The system of metro stations provoked new, more complex solutions to the communication nodes and transmodal cores of the city transport, as in the area of Ancient Serdica. A number of local and foreign developers and architects have contributed their expertise to Sofia's new scene. Meanwhile, some instances designed by a young generation of local architects have found international recognition.

Since the end of the 1980s Sofia's urbanism has followed a plurality, and, to a considerable degree, the local architecture scene has conformed with global tendencies. The external influences are clearly traceable in the city's history and deeply coded in the attitude of mind. Developments since the Liberation in 1878 have shown that Bulgarian capital is able to combine the numerous contradictory expressions resulting from various stages of synthesis. At the same time, these expressions accumulate effective integration strategies, which are both viable and capable of development.

View of Sofia from Vitosha Mountain

Photo: Tyuncher Eminov

View towards the Bulgarian National Bank and the Presidency building

At Crossroads

Georgi Stanishev

Sofia was born as a crossroads settlement linking east and west, north and south many centuries ago. Since then, hybridisation has run through its history. Different time periods, cultures, and architectures have filtered through into the body of the city, but one persistent characteristic has been the city's ability to hybridise flows and produce identity through the remixing of diverse influences. This is the fate of the periphery who experience cultural radiations from various centres: to construct novelty through reinterpretation.

This architectural guide blends architectural history and theory, criticism, and urban geography. It is conceived as an instrument in the hands of a curious traveller who is interested in architecture – not only in the form of monuments but also as everyday places, where the processes of past and present are still in action: markets, plazas, parks and gardens, inner courtyards between buildings, and other hidden treasures of Sofia's unique urbanity. The authors of this book give a chronology of the city's architectural history, but the guide is based on the geographic division of Sofia, so as to make walking, hiking, or wandering through the streets an adventure that mixes, in one glance, a medieval, Ottoman mosque, a structure influenced by Art Deco and National Romanticism, and a Bauhaus building.

Thus, although different pieces of the city have the scale and cultural typology of the dominant time of its construction, the most crucial parts are to be found in places where time has mixed different cultures, expressions, architecture, and lifestyles in an inseparable amalgam, blurring boundaries, crisscrossing languages, re-remixing lives and lifestyles. Because Sofia's space was always a marriage of the cultural flows stemming from powerful, influential centres throughout history – the Roman Empire, Byzantinum, and the Ottoman, Austro-Hungarian and Russian empires, to name but a few – the city has the status of a permanent periphery, a liberal and tolerant space where many influential vectors can be combined and remixed. This synthesis leads to innovation.

In the Bulgarian capital, to innovate does not mean to invent something new. To innovate means to recompose and hybridise. Sofia obtains the vitality of a hybrid city, or at least a city with typically hybrid places – places where the imprints of different times and cultures coexist in a dialogue. These places are composite ensembles of differences and times: they gather a variety of styles, typologies, and histories in one place.

This book catalogues these hybrid places based on geography rather than history, but multiple histories can be seen at single locations. A typical case in point is the so-called Square of Religious Tolerance the very centre of Sofia, which collects a mosque (Banya Bashi; 025), an Orthodox church (St Nedelya; 017), and a synagogue (the largest in the Balkans) in one plaza. Recently, in 2006, a new member of the company was added: a Catholic church (St Joseph).

Apart from spaces for worship and their monumental expressions, the other type of mixing machines in the city are the markets, which also form at crossroad junctions. Markets are live generators of the rhizomes that regulate city processes. One is featured in detail in this guide – the Central Covered Market (008) – and we also advise visits to others: the Women's Market, the main and oldest still-working agricultural free-trade square; Sitnyakovo local market, and the famous city-centre book-trading market on Slaveykov Square. At all these locations, visitors will experience Sofia's singular blend of vitality.

The Maps: Connecting History and Geography

This architectural guide to Sofia works on an intersection of historical and geographical principles. The sequence of the book's chapters follows the geographic articulation of the city territory. The centre of Sofia is represented by three maps – Central Core (CC), Centre to West (CW), and Centre to East (CE) – which cover the historic core of the city. Because of the high concentration of important architectural works from different periods of the city's development (from the 2nd century BCE to today), the centre is presented with maps with a larger scale.

The maps of the other zones are on a smaller scale, as their areas form a sort of periphery around the centre and basically correspond to the principle vectors of city growth: East, West, North, and South. These periphery areas are further divided into sub-areas (see key on bottom left of page 21). To a large extent, the geographic vectors correlate to the dominant intentions around at different periods in the city's history. For example, industrialisation in the 1920s and 1930s strongly developed the northern zone, while the era of communist rule subconsciously pushed the eastern vector of growth, establishing new, large-scale residential complexes. The recent period of restored democracy caused extension predominantly west- and southwards.

The points of interest and architectural objects profiled in the guide are marked with coloured boxes which contain the number of the project in the following catalogue. Besides the number and the geographical position, the boxes also signify the historical period to which the work belongs through their colour (see key on bottom right of page 21).

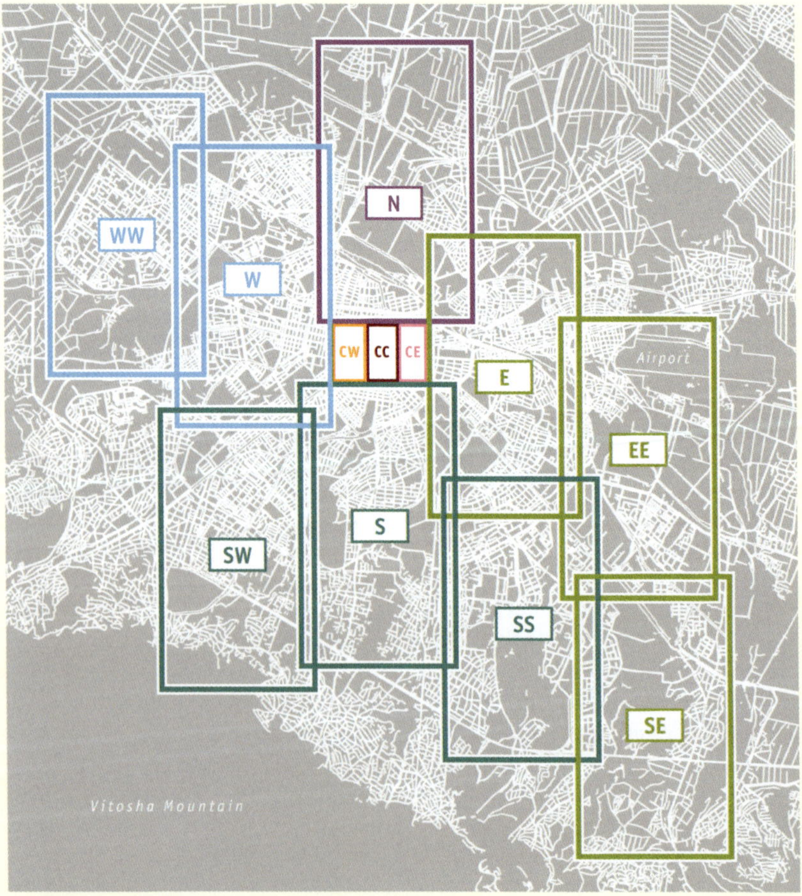

Outline of the maps seen over the territory of Sofia

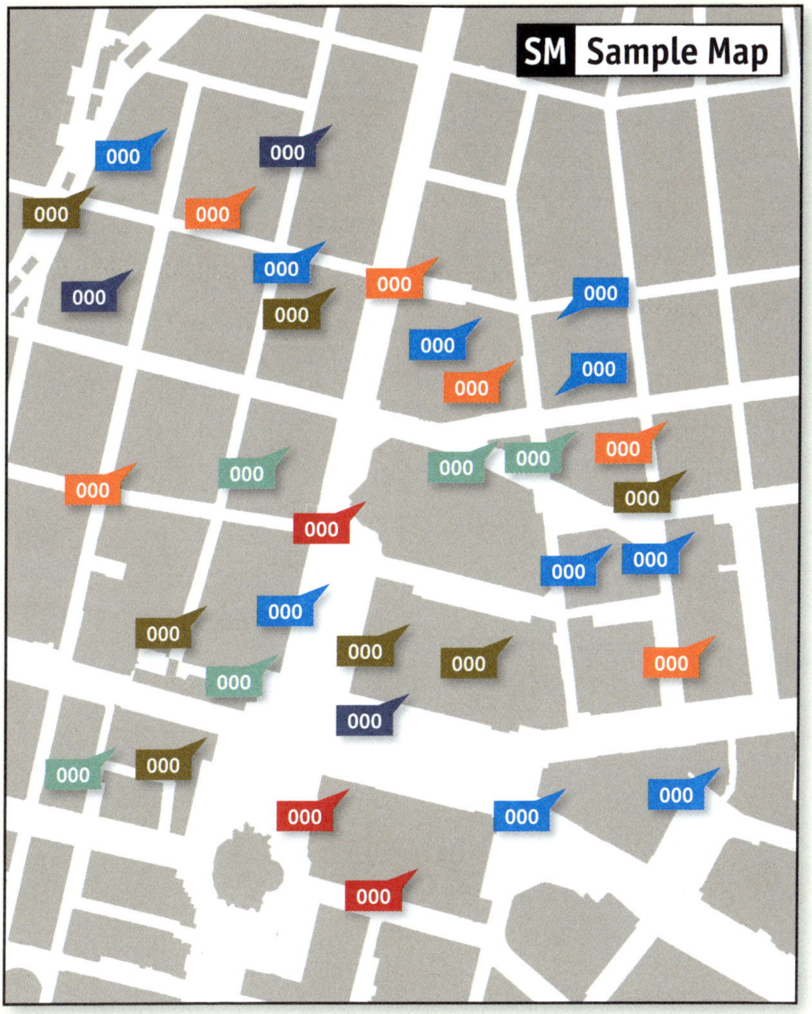

Geographical Zones

Zone	Codes
Central Core	CC
Centre to East	CE
Centre to West	CW
Eastern Zone	E, EE, SE
Southern Zone	S, SS, SW
Western Zone	W, WW
Northern Zone	N

Time Periods

- Antiquity and Byzantinum (6th century BCE–7th century CE)
- Medieval Bulgarian State (681–1376)
- Ottoman Empire (1376–1878)
- National Revival & Romanticism (1878–1920)
- Modernist Period (1920–1944)
- Communist Rule (1944–1989)
- Contemporary to the Present

Photograph of central Sofia, as seen in the map opposite

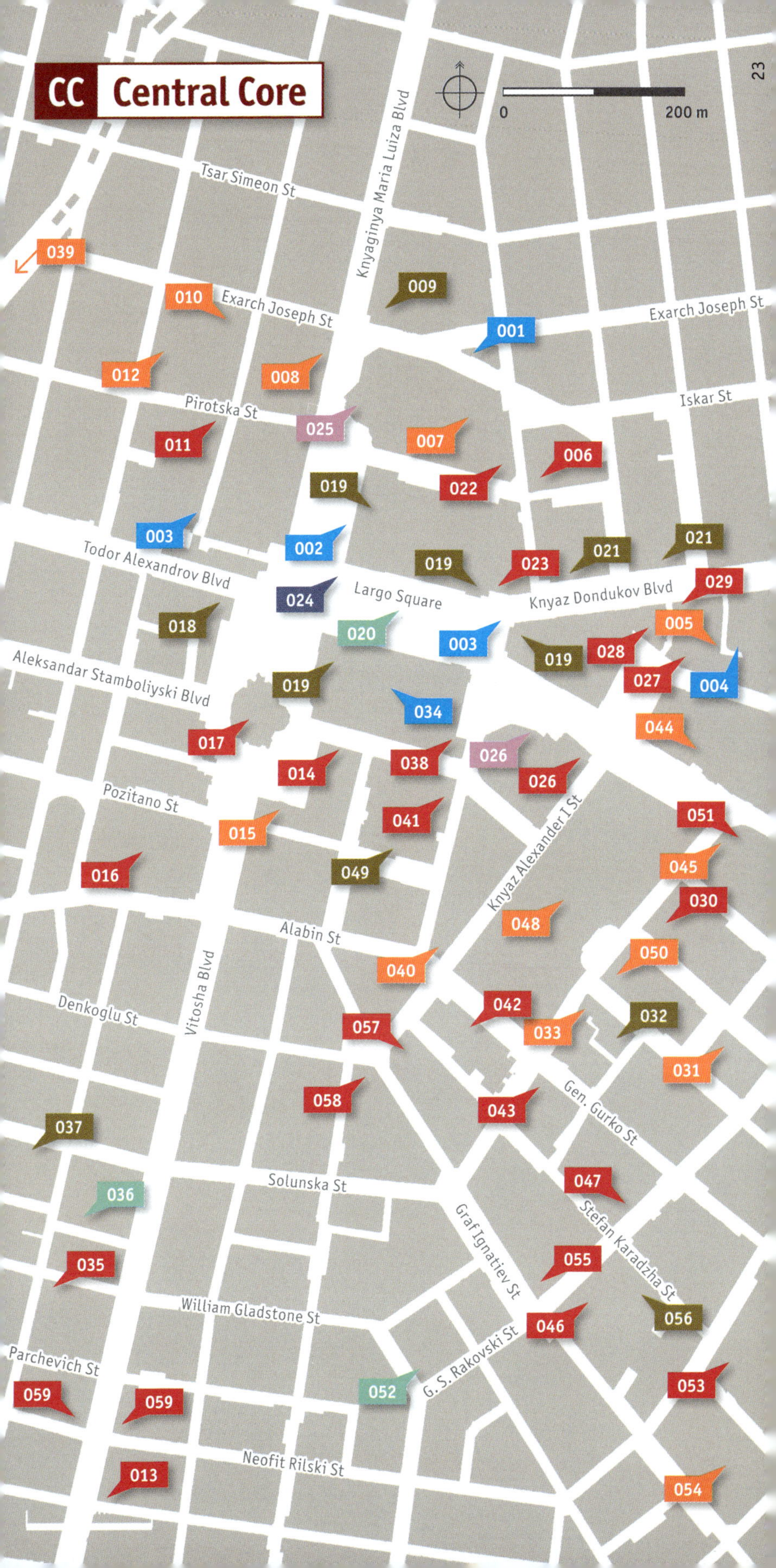
CC Central Core
0
200 m
Tsar Simeon St
Knyaginya Maria Luiza Blvd
Exarch Joseph St
Exarch Joseph St
Iskar St
Pirotska St
Todor Alexandrov Blvd
Largo Square
Knyaz Dondukov Blvd
Aleksandar Stamboliyski Blvd
Pozitano St
Knyaz Alexander I St
Alabin St
Vitosha Blvd
Denkoglu St
Gen. Gurko St
Solunska St
Graf Ignatiev St
Stefan Karadzha St
William Gladstone St
G. S. Rakovski St
Parchevich St
Neofit Rilski St
039
009
010
001
012
008
025
007
006
011
019
022
003
002
019
023
021
021
029
024
018
020
003
005
019
028
027
004
019
034
044
017
014
038
026
026
041
051
015
016
049
045
030
048
050
040
042
033
032
057
031
058
043
037
047
036
055
035
056
046
052
053
059
059
013
054

CE Centre to East

CW Centre to West

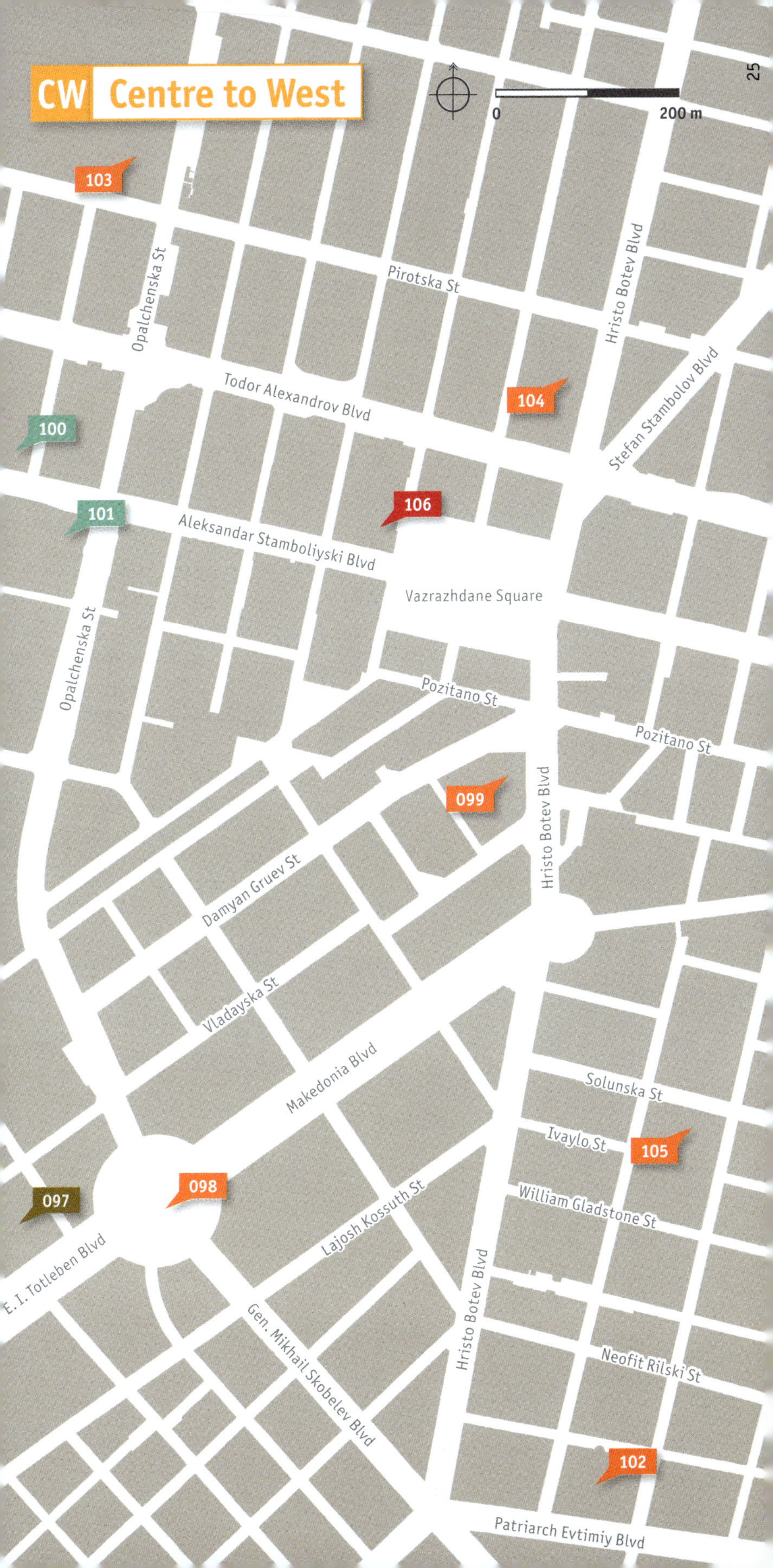

E Eastern Zone

EE Eastern Zone

SE Eastern Zone

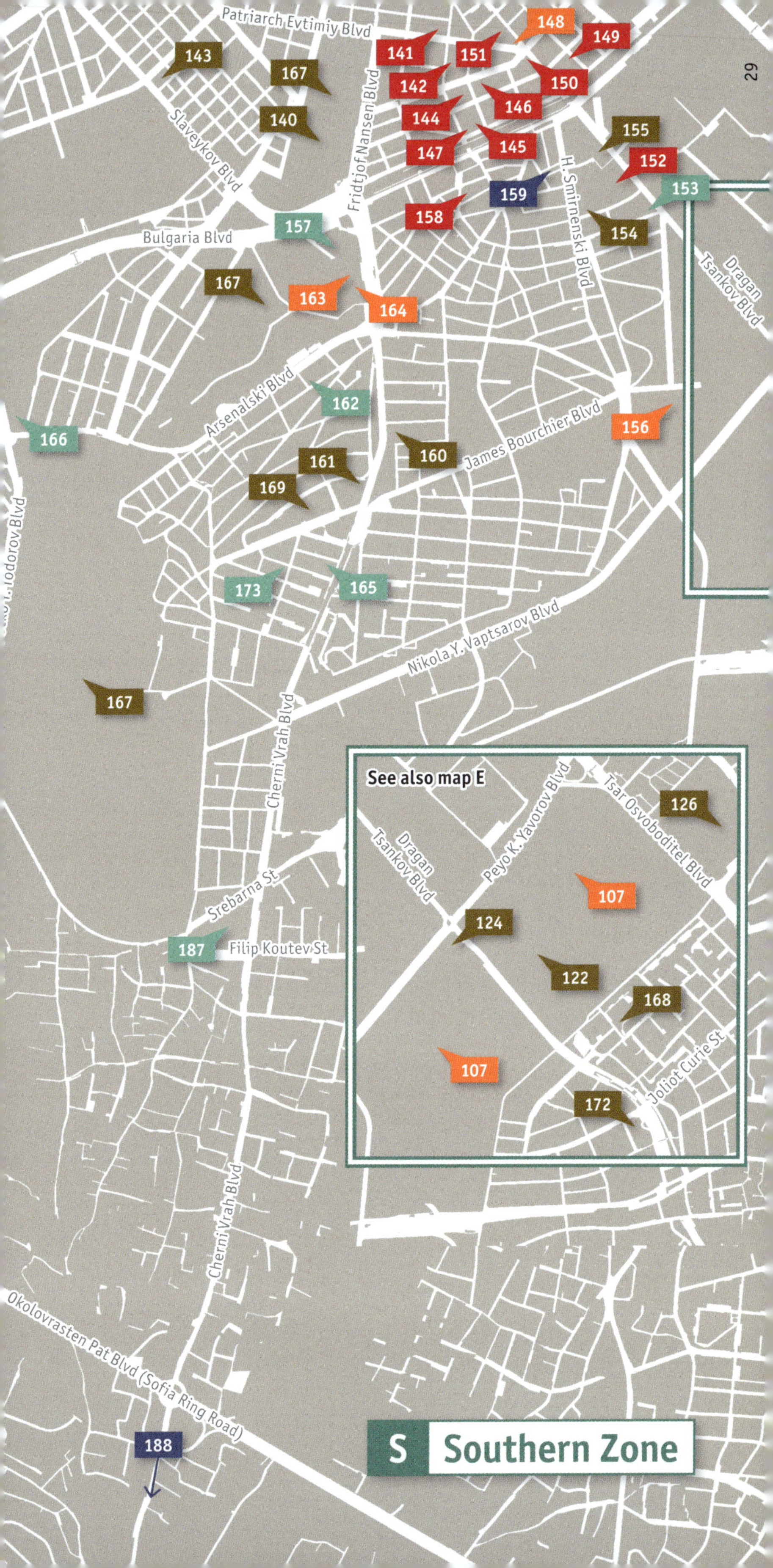
Patriarch Evtimiy Blvd
143
167
140
Slaveykov Blvd
Fridtjof Nansen Blvd
141
142
144
147
151
148
149
150
146
145
155
152
153
159
158
H. Smirnenski Blvd
154
Bulgaria Blvd
157
167
163
164
Dragan Tsankov Blvd
Arsenalski Blvd
162
166
156
James Bourchier Blvd
160
161
169
173
165
Nikola Y. Vaptsarov Blvd
167
Cherni Vrah Blvd
See also map E
Peyo K. Yavorov Blvd
Tsar Osvoboditel Blvd
126
Dragan Tsankov Blvd
107
124
122
168
Joliot Curie St
107
172
Srebarna St
187
Filip Koutev St
Cherni Vrah Blvd
Okolovrasten Pat Blvd (Sofia Ring Road)
188
S
Southern Zone

171
170
129
Tsar Osvoboditel Blvd
Dr G. M. Dimitrov Blvd
Nikola Gabrovski St
174
Prof. Marko Semov Blvd
185
8th December St
Akademik Stefan Mladenov St
Sveti Kliment Ohridski Blvd
Andrey Lyapchev Blvd
Aleksandar Malinov Blvd
Sveti Kliment Ohridski Blvd
Aleksandar Malinov Blvd
Okolovrasten Pat Blvd (Sofia Ring Road)
Okolovrasten Pat Blvd (Sofia Ring Road)
SS Southern Zone

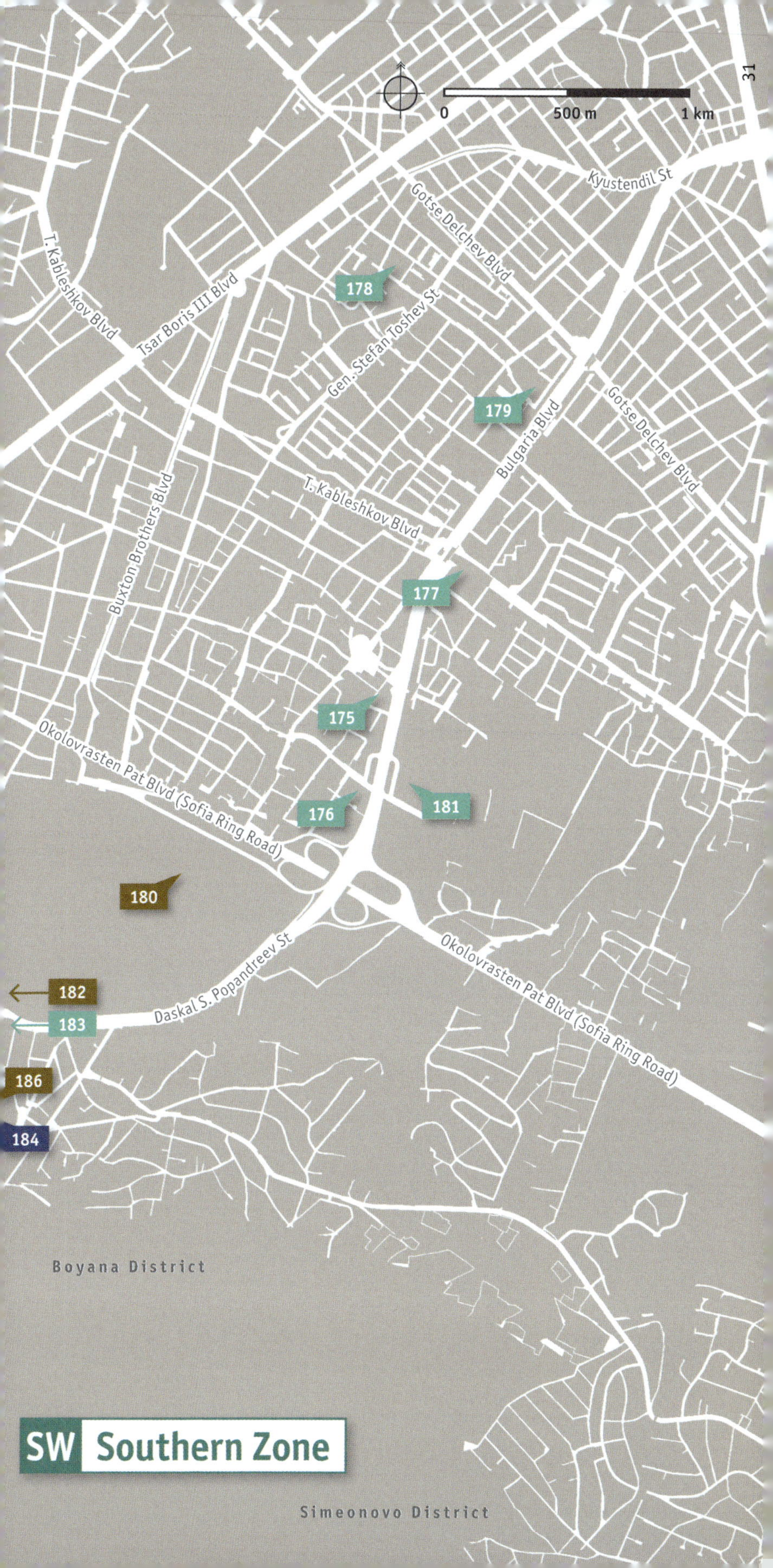
0
500 m
1 km
Kyustendil St
Gotse Delchev Blvd
T. Kableshkov Blvd
Tsar Boris III Blvd
178
Gen. Stefan Toshev St
179
Bulgaria Blvd
Gotse Delchev Blvd
T. Kableshkov Blvd
Buxton Brothers Blvd
177
175
Okolovrasten Pat Blvd (Sofia Ring Road)
176
181
180
Daskal S. Popandreev St
Okolovrasten Pat Blvd (Sofia Ring Road)
182
183
186
184
Boyana District
SW Southern Zone
Simeonovo District

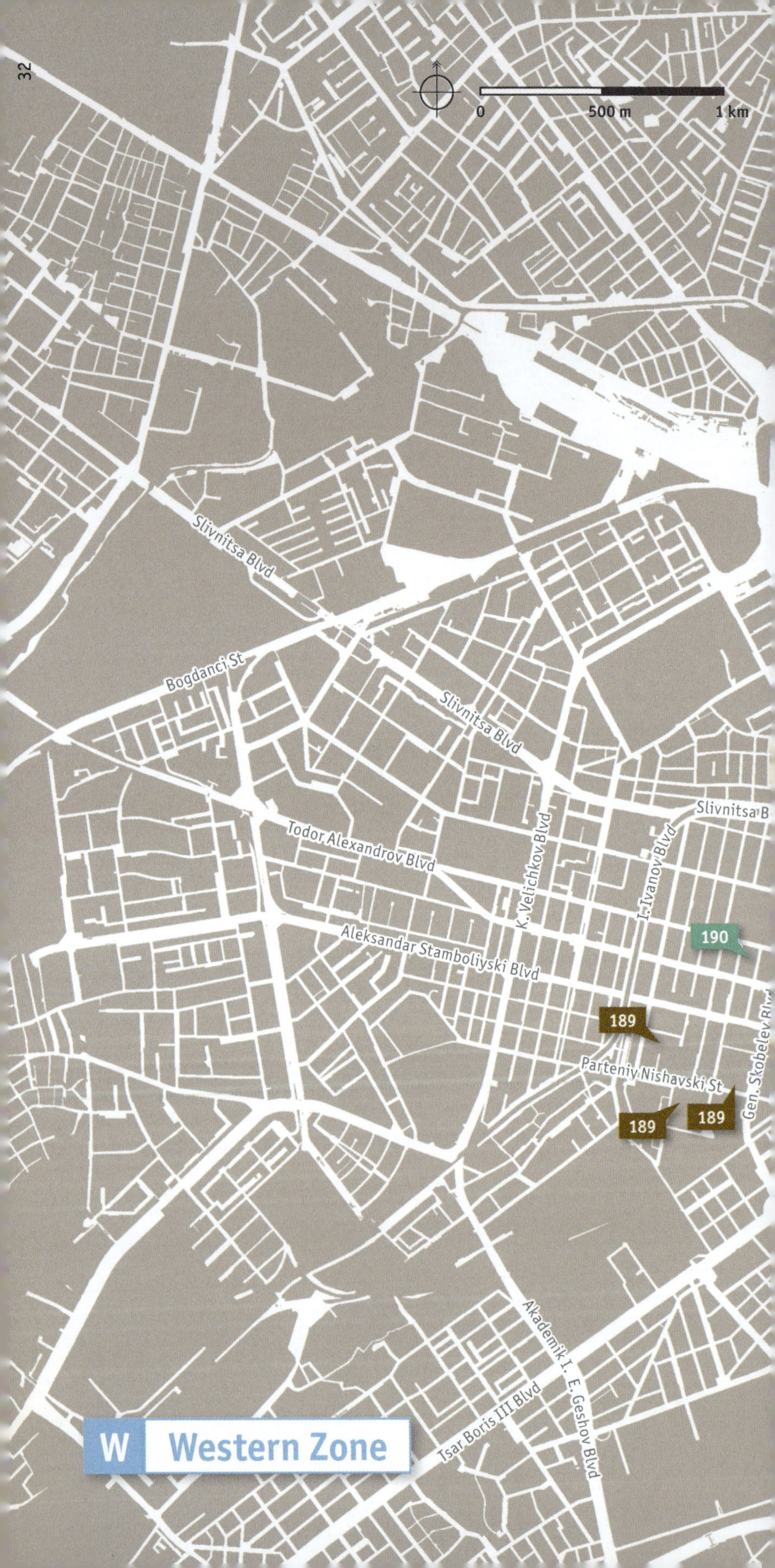
0
500 m
1 km
Slivnitsa Blvd
Bogdanci St
Slivnitsa Blvd
Slivnitsa B
Todor Alexandrov Blvd
K. Velichkov Blvd
I. Ivanov Blvd
Aleksandar Stamboliyski Blvd
190
189
Parteniy Nishavski St
189
189
Gen. Skobelev Blvd
Akademik I. E. Geshov Blvd
Tsar Boris III Blvd
W
Western Zone

0
500 m
1 km
Pancho Vladigerov Blvd
Tsaritsa Ioanna Blvd
Indira Gandi St
Dr Peter Dertliev Blvd
191
Suhodolska St
WW Western Zone

N Northern Zone

View towards the National Theatre (050), with the Ministry of Defence (030) at the bottom of the picture, and Ministry of Internal Affairs (053), with the St Sedmochislenitsi Church (054) – top part of the image

Central Core

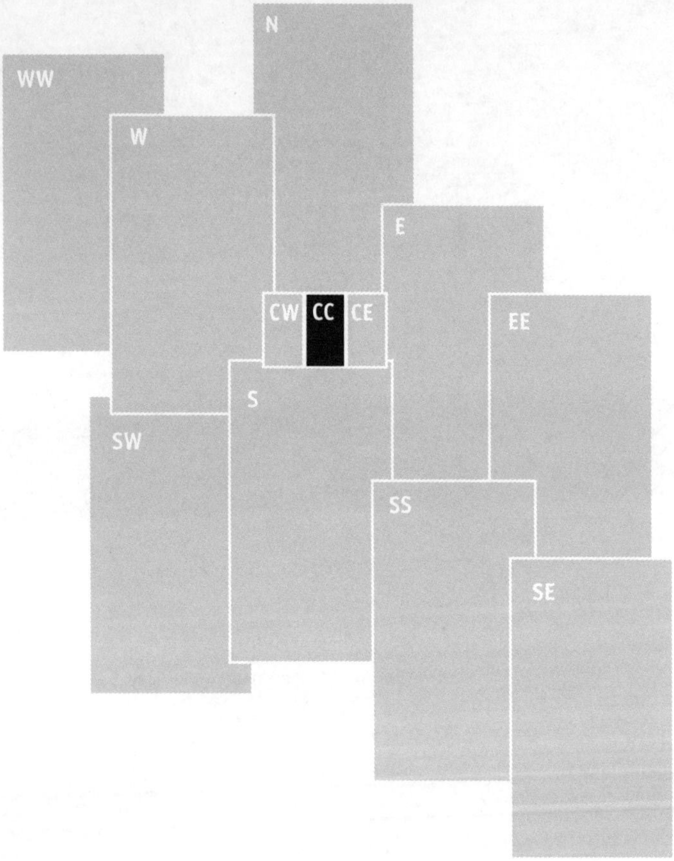

Map CC

The pluralist way of thinking about the local people can be traced back to the activities of the manifold population of the Antique and medieval city. The location was populated by the Thracian tribe of the Serds from the 8th century BCE onwards, and known as Serdonopolis or Civitas Serdensium. The regulation and fortification of Roman Serdica started in the 1st century BCE. After that, the history of the city, which was the capital of the provinces Dacia Aureliana and Dacia Mediterranea, was connected to the names of a number of emperors and rulers. Two very important documents were proclaimed in Serdica and Triadica, as the city later became known: the Edict of Toleration (311) and the Doctrine of the Saint Trinity, enacted by the Council of Serdica (343–344). The city was conquered by the Bulgarians on 9 April 809 and renamed Sredets. It was the seat of a patriarch, and in the 12th century it became a metropolitan seat and a centre of the spiritual community of the Small Holy Mountain of Serdica, which, at the end of the 14th century, consisted of about 100 monasteries. In that natural, spiritual, political, and military context, the plan and the spatial composition of the city, with its surrounding spiritual and transportational infrastructure, were established throughout Antiquity and the Middle Ages. These conservative elements of urbanisation have shown their resilience, left important traces, and had a significant impact upon the development and formation of the modern core of Sofia.

Hot Mineral Water Spring
Banski Square
4th century BCE,
2nd–1st century BCE,
1st–6th century CE

001

CC

The spring was the initial motivation for the development of the settlement that is now Sofia, over the last eight millenniums. The first written sources about the spring date from Early Antiquity. The spring is located south of the Banya Bashi Mosque, but not marked in the contemporary place (see number 12 on the map on page 41). It was captured by the Romans in the 2nd–1st century BCE. Since then, the location has been a focal point for functions related to the uses of its mineral water. Some fragments of a Roman thermae from the 4th century and a Turkish hammam from the 16th century are preserved nearby. The Public Mineral Baths (nowadays the Regional History Museum) and a number of fountains were built at the beginning of the 20th century. A public space with new sources and the figure of Apollo Medicus were designed in 2002 by Stanislav Konstantinov and Georgi Chapkanov. Over the centuries the spring has developed a semantic value, which has progressed from its function to being a symbol of the city. It can be seen on antique coins and the Sofia coat of arms. Today

it is one of the liveliest places in the city centre. Access to the spring and its waters is free, and people queue with plastic bottles and large containers to collect the valuable 37-degrees Centigrade mineral water and take it home. Individuals of all ages and social strata can be seen here: pensioners, sporty family drivers climbing out of the latest Mercedes, workers from Sofia's suburbs and surrounding villages, and many others besides. Young and old, rich and poor, and people of all faiths: everyone crowds around the pipes. The spring is a truly democratic spot that bridges the cultural traditions of the city, from ancient times to the present day.

Streets and insulas of ancient Serdica

1st–6th century BCE

002

CC

The first settlements on the site of the present-day Sofia Valley are believed to have been founded by the Thracian tribes dominated by the Serds. Around the 2nd century BCE, the area was conquered by the Romans under the rule of Tiberius. Urban life in Roman Serdica was organised into quarters (insulas) and public spaces, defined by the orthogonal street grid. The pattern was based on the planning system devised by Hippodamus in 5th century BCE Greece. The grid of secondary streets was arranged around the two main streets of the Roman city: the east–west Decumanus Maximus (see number 1 on page 41) and the north–south Cardo Maximus (2). This street network existed until the end of the 14th century. The scale and the main public spaces corresponded to the status of the city. Serdica's Decumanus Maximus was 6.5 metres wide and in the 6th century was picturesquely covered with large stone plates. The perspective, when entering from the Eastern Gate, was defined by 2.1-metre-wide pedestrian passways with an imposing colonnade. The living standard in the insulas was defined by the scale of the secondary streets, the decumani and cardines covered with stone plates. The basic infrastructure for the water supply and the canal system was set underneath the street. Because of the limited and unchangeable fortifications and streets, the insulas have survived a number of internal metamorphoses over 12 centuries. Some important fragments of the two main streets and the insulas were exposed under Nezavisimost Square and Knyaginya Maria Luiza Boulevard (3) (Vassil Kitov, Yuliy Farkov, Slavey Galabov, Krassen Andreev, Hristo Genchev, 2015). The excavation and exhibition of the inner-city insulas began in the middle of the 1950s with the reconstruction of Sofia city centre. The first important fragment of archaeological remains was preserved in the court of the Sheraton Hotel and the Presidential Office, both built in 1954–1956. The complex rose around the St George Rotunda (4), which was probably part of the Roman forum complex (5), situated to the west of it and facing the Cardo Maximus. The partly researched but not exposed forum is 42 x 65 metres. The remains of the Bouleuterion (6) located on the Cardo Maximus were documented, but no longer exist. A street with a width of 9.8 metres, located south of the rotunda, was studied. Some parts of the street were preserved under the contemporary covering. The scale of the street is evidence of its urban importance. The road was a public space linking the forum to some important objects for spiritual life and power. The remains of a public building from the 4th century,

similar to the rotunda concerning its composition and size, is exposed east of it. From the 13th to 17th centuries, the building was changed several times (7). A large housing complex with mosaics was discovered in the south-east (8). It is thought to be a residence of Constantine the Great (306–337). The building was used as the seat of the local rulers, including Sevastocrator Kaloyan. Some remains are preserved below an office building but are not accessible to visitors. Three medieval churches, which are closely related to the history and function of the complex, are located nearby: the St Nikolay Chudotvorec court complex chapel (9) from the 12th century; St Paraskeva Church (10), dedicated to St Petka Paraskeva the Bulgarian, built around 1240; and the St Petka Samarzhiyska Church (11) from the 11th and 14th–15th centuries. During the next five centuries of Ottoman rule, the city changed radically. Its compositional and building structures were destroyed. Some antique and medieval remains were preserved by chance under the current city level and form a complicated cultural stratigraphy. The remains are the object of a 60-year policy for their continuous integration into the contemporary urban space.

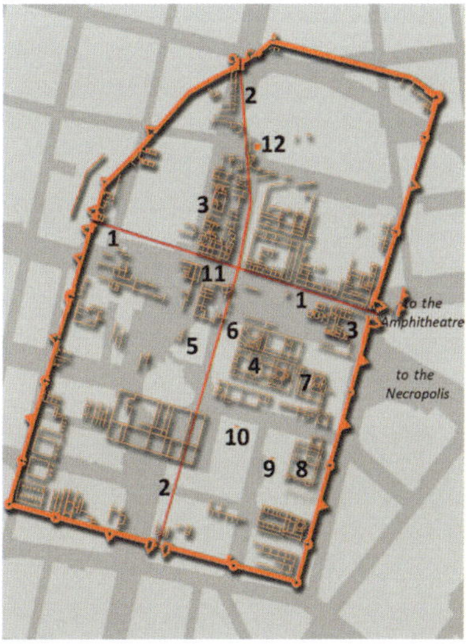

Ancient fortification system

2nd–6th century CE

The first fortification wall of Serdica (3 on the map on page 43) was built from 176 to 180 CE, during the reign of Marcus Aurelius and his son Commodus, and enclosed an area of 338 metres east–west to 562 metres north–south, or 17 hectares. The necropolis (2) and the amphitheatre (1) were located outside the wall, a short distance from the Eastern Gate. Two fragments of the first wall are preserved next to the south tower of the Eastern Gate and in the basement of the Halite Central Market. The 2-metre-thick and 8–9-metre-high brickwork (*Opus latericium*) wall stood on a stone base. The fortification was rebuilt in the first half of the 3rd century in brick and stone strata (*Opus mixtum*). The wall was enlarged to a thickness of 2.15 metres and a height of 10–12 metres. Some round towers were added, and in these parts the width of the wall increased to up to 4.2 metres, including the stairs. In 270–337, the city extended to cover 75–80 hectares. A second wall was constructed with an irregular, extended to the north configuration, reflecting the topography and the road. It was made from river stones of varying sizes (*Opus incertum*), had a thickness of 2.85 metres on a 3.3–3.7-metre-wide base, and was strengthened with towers of different shapes. The walls were reconstructed during the reign of Justinian I, in the middle of the 6th century. The inner wall – brickwork on a stone base – was widened 1.8 metres and raised. A second wall (*Proteihisma*), with a thickness of 1.6–2.9-metres, was built a distance of 20 metres outside the first (4). That configuration of the fortifications was preserved until the 14th century, when it was destroyed by the Ottomans. The Western (6) and Eastern (5) gates, which defined the Decumanus Maximus, as well as some fragments from different historical periods, were conserved and exposed in accessible open and covered spaces. The Eastern Gate, which led to Serdica's necropolis and eventually to Constantinople, was discovered and exposed in the course of the realisation of an underground pedestrian passway (Gancho Ganchev, Ivan Boyadjev, Stefan Boyadjiev) in 1966–1971. This was the first meaningful urban intervention that showed the potential of Antique heritage for the development of underground urbanism, and a forerunner of integrated conservation. The large scale of the stonework added to the inner and outer gates in the 6th century (*Opus quadratum*), and the brickwork pentagonal towers deserve attention. The fragmentary conservation and open-air exposition of the Western Gate was accomplished in 2016 (Yordanka Kandulkova, Valentin Todorov). Then parts of the Decumanus Maximus, some structures from the 2nd–3rd and 6th centuries CE of the 4.5-metre-thick wall, and the street leading to it (Via Sagularis), as well as a triangular and a pentagonal tower, were exposed. It is supposed

that the Ottomans destroyed the fortification segment and forcibly entered the city in 1382. The Northern Gate (7) is preserved under the point at which Knyaginya Maria Luiza Boulevard and Exarch Joseph Street cross. The gate's construction is identical to that of the other gates, but it shows a different planning scheme. The round tower (8) on the north-west wall corner (Iskar/Serdica streets) has a diameter of 22 metres. The characteristics of the structure correspond to those from the 3rd and 6th centuries. The tower was covered with stone blocks and received its orthogonal configuration in the 13th century. A triangular brickwork tower (9) on a stone base from the 6th century and a wall fragment are preserved and exposed in the basement of the office building at 16 Knyaginya Maria Luiza Boulevard (Milko Pindev, 1960). The tower is today an accent in a multifunctional cultural space (Donika Georgieva, Miroslav Velkov, 2017). Some wall segments from the 3rd–4th and 6th centuries (10) are conserved and exposed in the basement of the Central Market. Some pieces of the same wall with a round tower, parts of the Via Sagularis, and remains of the St Spas Church from the 11th–13th century, as well as some medieval structures, are preserved under the Bulbank building (11). The fragments include some streets and insula. The ruins can be observed from the corner of Todor Alexandrov Boulevard and Knyaz Boris I Street. The path of the southern wall was identified by recovered pieces. The supposed location of the Southern Gate (12) is under buildings on Vitosha Boulevard.

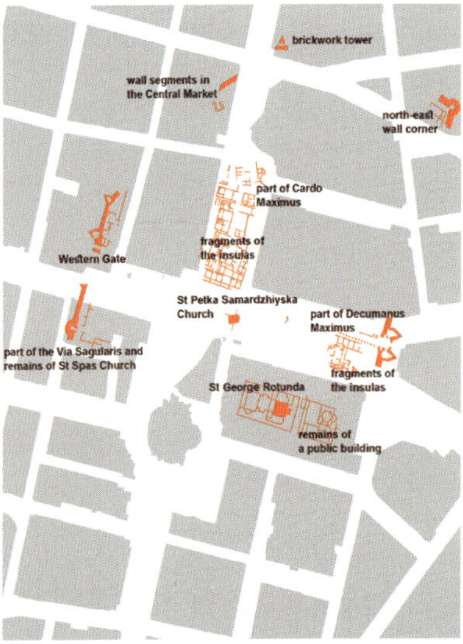

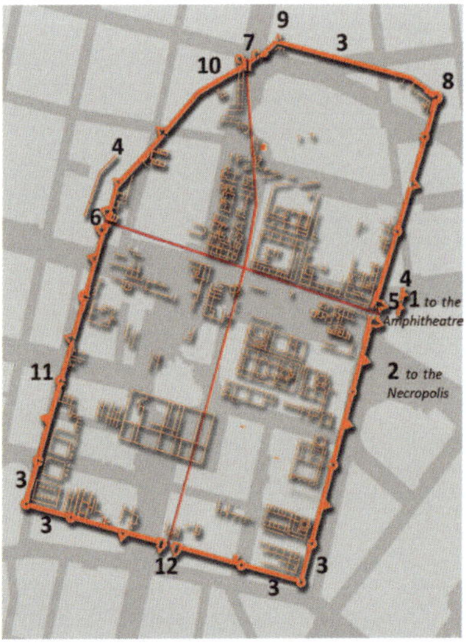

Amphitheatre of Serdica ↓

004

CC

2–4 Budapest Street
Partial exposition:
Petko Marinov, Konstantin Peev
3rd–4th century CE, 2007

The Roman Theatre and the Amphitheatre occupy neighbouring locations at the foot of the northern slope of the Sofia 'sacral hill', east of the Roman city. The theatre was built in the end of the 2nd century, while the amphitheatre was constructed during the reign of Diocletian (284–305) and then enlarged during the reign of Constantine I the Great (324–337). The amphitheatre lost its initial meaning after the imposition of Christianity by Theodosius I the Great, and it started to be used for elementary pragmatic purposes. The amphitheatre was discovered in 2004 during the construction of the Arena di Serdica Hotel and is today partially exposed in its foyer. The integration of the Antique remains in the new architecture consistently followed the principles of clear image separation, as opposed to running according to a postmodern creative interpretation.

Goethe Institute – Bulgaria (former rental building) ↑

005

CC

1 Budapest Street
Reconstruction:
Hristo Ganchev, Ivan Velikov
1885, 1904, 2003 (reconstruction)

The edifice was built in 1885 by a foundation run by Dr Nikola Vassiliadi. Vassiliadi, who studied medicine in Athens, Paris and Berlin, was an activist during the Bulgarian National Revival and a donor to the Bulgarian educational system. For a long period the building was used for educational and administrative purposes, and in 2003 the Goethe Institute moved in. The contemporary usage fully corresponds to the tradition and spirit of the location. In the course of the reconstruction, the authentic Secession design of the façade was preserved. The valuable elements of the interior, such as the staircases, foyers, hall, and mosaics, were successfully adapted, because of the rational plan of the building. The functional structure of the service rooms was maintained and the basement and loft were optimally used for new rooms, and a better inner flexibility was achieved. A new wing with classrooms connects the building with the inner court.

Musala apartment building

006
CC

12 Serdica Street
Kosta Nikolov
1925, 1949

This building initially contained shops on the ground level, and then offices and apartments on the upper floors, arranged around a corridor. The structure was damaged by bombardments in the Second World War, and in the course of its rebuilding in 1949 the upper-floor offices were converted to flats. The edifice is one of the first attempts in the field of the cooperative housing developments in Bulgaria. Its façade is vertically structured through densely-ordered pilaster strips with slim windows between them. The grandeur of the building is heightened by a tower that accentuates the corner, crowned by monumental sculptural compositions. The architecture presents a transitional phase from art nouveau to the monumental classicism of the 1930s. This stylistic mixture makes the building one of the earliest art-deco works in Bulgaria, as well as one of the earliest in the Balkans.

View towards the Sofia Regional History Museum (former Public Mineral Baths; 007) and Banya Bashi Mosque (025)

Sofia Regional History Museum (former Public Mineral Baths) 007 CC

1 Banski Square

Emil von Foerster, 1893. Project revisions: Yanaki Samardjiev, 1895; Friedrich Grünanger, Petko Momchilov, 1904; Petko Momchilov, Yordan Milanov. Plastic elements, ceramics, and decoration: Haralampi Tachev, Stefan Dimitrov. Carpentry: Hristo Krystev. Adaptation: Stanislav Konstantinov, Alexandar Genchev, Iglika Liudckanova, 2014.

At the end of the 19th century, the idea emerged to erect a public mineral bathhouse next to the mineral water spring, which, with its central location, formed the very heart of Sofia. An international architectural competition was announced. The project passed through several revisions, until in 1908 a small public baths was inaugurated. Five years later a larger building with an institute for water cures was opened to the south of it. The small public baths were destroyed during the Second World War. In 1998 the Municipality of Sofia decided to adapt the building to the needs of the Regional History Museum, which was inaugurated in 2015. In the course of the adaptation, both the plan and the elevations of the original building were restored. The Baths, as it is known by Sofia's citizens, is one of the masterpieces of the Secession, and was

also strongly influenced by Bulgarian National Romanticism. Regarded in the European context, it proves a tendency to break with the initial cosmopolitan ideas of the avant-garde and to individualise aesthetic concepts. The architecture successfully combines a clear tectonic structure with Secession decoration, arranged in a symmetrical baroque plan. The sensitivity in the ceramic figure drawings is reminiscent of Alfons Mucha. The story hidden in the drawings is the divine quality of the water and its meaning for the city. The drinking fountains on the façades create a semantic link between the internal function of the building with its public space, thus exposing the consistency of its *genius loci*. Dominated by the Byzantine artistic system, but also adopting other cultural influences, the building's unique semantic and aesthetic mixture elevates it to one of the most emblematic objects in Sofia. The temple of water and symbol of the city has embraced its new role following the historic civil metamorphoses. It tells the city's two-millennium history under the whispering of the preserved fountains, the gaze of Apollo Medicus, Ulpia Serdica, and the image of a mysterious woman.

Halite Central Market

008

CC

25 Knyaginya Maria Luiza Blvd
Naum Torbov.
Artworks: Haralambi Tachev.
Stonecutter: Georgi Kiselinchev.
Reconstruction and restoration: Konstantin Antonov, Hristo Ganchev, Adriana Kantardjieva
1911, 2000 (restoration)

The building is one of the highlights of Bulgarian architecture and sculpture from the beginning of the 20th century. It is a three-nave hall with an area of 3,200 square metres, which forms the western part of the architectural frame of Banski Square. The location had previously been used as a market and public space. The architectural style combines local medieval aesthetics, as shown in the massive outer walls, with the slender free-standing double columns of the iron structure. The coloured sculptural façade decoration is a skilful Secessionist interpretation of Byzantine art. The clock tower is a typical element that shaped public space in the National Revival period in the 18th and 19th centuries. The renunciation of traditional compositional schemes, along with the modern roof structure and artistic language create an integral architecture. In the course of the adaptation, the original features of the building were restored. The use of space was optimised through an additional underground level and two second-floor galleries. A new fountain was built in the hall's centre, following the author's original idea, as in the plans from 1909. The clockwork from 1911, produced by H. Aron, Berlin, was restored and exposed at the end of the main hall. Remains of the Antique fortifications,

from the 3rd–4th and 6th centuries, were conserved and exposed in the underground floor, along with the remnants of an intramural Antique bath from the 4th century. The route of the fortification wall is marked on the flooring and pavement inside and outside the Halls. In this way, contemporaneity and the past coexist in a lively urban context. The conservation and exposition of archaeological heritage restores the presence of essential ancient and medieval elements of the city as part of its various and enriching strata.

Mixed-use residential and commercial building

009
CC

16 Knyaginya Maria Luiza Blvd/
27 Exarch Joseph Street
Milko Pindev
1960

This mixed-use building makes its mark through its distinctive shape and its thirteen-storey tower which dominates the crossroads. The ground floor is set back from the street, leaving a colonnaded public space. The lower section of the structure, consisting of three storeys and a basement, was initially planned for the Sofia History Museum, because one of the corner towers of the Antique fortifications is exposed in the basement. The level below ground and the two first floors were connected by a freestanding staircase, forming a recognisable museum space. The impressive original interior was later turned into shops and offices, and the storeys were separated. In 2017 access to the archaeological remains in the basement was restored and a museum exhibition was organised.

דע לפני מי אתה עומד

Central Synagogue
18 Exarch Joseph Street
Friedrich Grünanger
1909, 2009

010
CC

The Central Synagogue is the biggest Sephardic synagogue in Europe and the third biggest of all Jewish temples on the continent. It replaced the old synagogue, Ahava i Hesed ('Love and Goodness'), on the same spot. With its area of 659 square metres, it can hold up to 1,300 visitors. The building was extensively damaged by bombing during the Second World War, when the famous Jewish Library burned and a large share of the valuable books were lost. The synagogue is still the spiritual centre of the Jewish community in the Bulgaria, a community which was already established in the 10th century, at the time of the First Bulgarian State. In the 15th century the community was joined by Jews from Germany, Catalonia, and Aragon. The historic stratification of the cultural influences that followed the migration is reflected in the architectural language of the synagogue. The synagogue is a symmetrical building, dominated by an imposing polygonal dome with a height of 23 metres and a diameter of 19 metres. The central space is enriched with four niches and four conches, all arched, corresponding with the eight segments of the dome. The coloured skylight of the dome and its external appearance remind one of central skylights in churches from the Renaissance. The design follows the Byzantine decorative system and consists of alternating belts of ceramic tiles and plaster, complemented by typical Moorish architectural, sculptural, and decorative elements. The same architectural language is continuously developed throughout the domes, towers, frontispieces, and interior details. The specific plastic form of the dome successfully links its large volume to the delicate ornamentation of the walls. Multiple cultural links are embedded in this unique building. The context of the growing interest in Oriental arts and their Secessionist interpretation in European art at the time is clearly perceivable. In that sense, the Central Synagogue can be defined as one of the highlights of National Romanticism.

← Lawyers Union and Cultural House

011

CC

7 Pirotska Street

Sava Ovcharov, Yordan Yordanov

1928

The design of the building was the outcome of an international competition. It serves as the central place for professional, social, and cultural meetings of the legal community. The façades are designed with various window openings: rectangular, round, single- and double-arched. On the one hand, this diversity disturbs the façades' unity, but on the other, it creates an original dissonance. The corner-tower wall and the window frames are visually strengthened by the stone cladding. Worthy of interest are the main entrance, the large coat of arms, and the medallions of justice.

← Holy Trinity Romanian Church 012 CC

152 Knyaz Boris Street

Friedrich Grünanger.

Wall paintings: Vermont, Artakino, Serafim; 1912

This church was built with donations from Romanian emigrants and funding from the Romanian State. The church has a cross-dome structure with a central dome and two bell-towers that flank the narthex. The architectural language is a mixture of neo-Byzantine and neo-Romanesque features. The twin-arched windows and the precisely crafted details remind one of the Romanian Renaissance in the 18th century. With Byzantine columns and arches, covered by three domes, the entrance is conspicuous. The building is an accent in the street silhouette and an example of the neo-historical stylistic searches in Orthodox Church expression around 1900. It is stylistically related to the Residence of the Romanian King's Legation, built in 1933. In the same period the architect Friedrich Grünanger designed the building for the former Romanian Institute to the Romanian King's Legation on 12 Exarch Joseph Street as a part of the church's ensemble.

Cooperative apartment building ↑ 013 CC

63 Vitosha Boulevard

Vasko Vassilev

1946

Located at the point where a now-pedestrian boulevard crosses a smaller street, the building was planned before the Second World War and possesses all the characteristics of the local modernist language from that period. The compact architecture is well proportioned and structured alongside the boulevard and the street through horizontal strips of windows interrupted by small verandas. The window ledges run continuously and pop out of the front surface. The rounded shape of the corner is completed by the curved lines of the canopy and the eaves. The strips end in small verandas, which create deep shadows and serve as transitions to the puristic north part of the façade. The elegant proportions of the building are enhanced by the different treatment of the last floor, with its recession in the north crowned by a pergola. The generosity of space is continued in the plans of the apartments and the interior of the staircase.

Seat of the Bishop of Sofia and office building

014
CC

6 Sveta Nedelya Square/
7 Tsar Kaloyan Street
Seat of the Bishop of Sofia:
Panteley Tsvetkov
1932
Office building:
Mara Zaharieva, Stoyan Bosolov
1934

This complex consists of the Seat of the Bishop in the eastern wing, and an office building oriented to St Nedelya Square in the west. The plain façades, structured by strictly ordered windows, appear almost minimalist today. These clear areas serve as a quiet backdrop for the striking corner, where a slim column stretches four floors, finishing with a small arch. The entire building is clad in local limestone. A modest entrance on Saborna Street leads to a church devoted to St Petka Paraskeva the Bulgarian, located in the basement of the building. It was founded in 1257 by the ruler of the province of Sredets, Sevastokrator Kaloyan. The church was destroyed in 1386, but according to the traveller Stefan Gerlach, it was rebuilt in the 16th century. It was incorporated into the modern building by preserving its initial, single-space character. The eastern part is a three-storey building. An opening of the front with three arches leads through the inner court to a three-nave anteroom. The complex has an individual formal language – poetic rationalism mixed with National Romanticism.

Theological Faculty of Sofia University (former St Kliment Ohridski Theological Academy)

015
CC

19 Sveta Nedelya Square
Friedrich Grünanger,
Karl Heinrich.
Decoration: Haralampi Tachev.
Wall paintings: Nikola Ganushev, Gospodin Jelyazkov, Nikola Marinov, Ivan Belkovski, Nikolay Rostovcev. Stone sculptures: Richard Hardy, Angelo Filotti
1914, 1923 (decoration)

The construction of the building began in 1908 and was completed in 1914. During the First World War the structure was used as a military hospital. In 1923 the Theological Academy opened there, and since then the building has been the centre for disseminating Orthodox knowledge. Today it also houses the National Museum of Church History and Archaeology of the Holy Synod, the library of the Bulgarian Patriarchy, and a chapel. The building is an emblematic example of National Romanticism as it reinterprets and mixes medieval Byzantine traditions with National Revival architecture from the 18th and 19th centuries. The strong influence of the Viennese Secession, and in particular of Otto Wagner, is evident in the decoration of the building. Large columns create a deep perspective in the entrance foyer and lead to a baroque staircase at the far end. While the interior's tectonic has a classicist appearance, its decor persistently inclines towards art nouveau.

Courthouse

016

CC

2 Vitosha Boulevard

Pencho Koychev, Petar Zagorski, Georgi Papazov. Sculptures: Lyubomir Dalchev, Kiril Shivarov, Lyuben Dimitrov. Frescoes: Dechko Uzunov. Stained glass and mosaics: Ivan Penkov. Iron and bronze elements: Baevi brothers; 1928–1940. Lion figures: Velichko Minekov; 1985. Reconstruction: Liubomir Semerdjiev.

1940, 2007 (reconstruction)

The Courthouse, with its 8,500 square metres of built area, was the first building of such a large size in the centre of Sofia. As it occupies a whole urban block, it exerts a significant impact upon the development of the neighbouring area. The architectural design corresponds to the size of the street spaces that limit the block. When regarded in detail, the imposing classicist front towards the boulevard reveals some Byzantine and Romanesque influences. The secondary street-fronts have a more rational and simply structured design. The general composition of the building follows functional expediency, despite the prestigious accessways that pass through the impressive central interior spaces. The cellular

structure of alternating court halls and smaller spaces is arranged around eight inner courts that bring in natural light and ventilation. The rational structure appears in the classicist character of the interior, which is richly decorated with works of art: stained glass, sculptures, wall paintings, mosaics, and architectural details. The synthesis of the plastic and fine arts integrates neoclassical and modernist trends, and defines the building as one of the masterpieces of art deco in Bulgaria. The thematic of the works of art forms a specific gallery of the eternal symbols of truth and justice: a flat relief showing the court of King Solomon in the 10th century BCE; a mosaic of the goddess of justice, Themis; a flat relief and a wall painting dedicated to the severe Bulgarian law-giving practices during the reign of Khan Krum in the 9th century; stained glass showing the scales of the balanced, wise, and fair solution; the lion, as the basic sign of the Bulgarian State and of power and courage. In the period from 1980 to 1998, part of the building was used by the National Museum of History. Today the original function of the Courthouse has been restored.

View of St Nedelya Church. The Cardo Maximus and Decumanus of Ancient Serdica were once located 100 metres to the north of the square.

St Nedelya Church (St Kral Church)

017

CC

20 Sveta Nedelya Square
Reconstruction, rehabilitation: Nikola Lazarov. New building: Ivan Vasilyov, Dimitar Tsolov. Frescoes: Nikolay Rostovtsev and team
10th century, 1901 and 1920 (reconstructions),
1933 (new building), 1973 (frescoes)

In 1856 Sultan Abdul-Mejid issued a *Hatt-i humayun* which gave religious liberty to Christians in the Ottoman Empire. This event was immediately followed by the erection of a new, monumental church in the centre of Sofia. The new edifice replaced the medieval church, dedicated to the Holy and Great Martyr Kyriaki (Dominica) of Nicomedia, dated to the 10th century. As the relics of the Serbian king St Stefan Uroš II Milutin (1282–1321) were treasured there, the church was also known as St Kral ('Holy King'). The medieval church constructed by native masters was a three-nave basilica with proportions of 35.5 × 19 metres – rather impressive for the time. The church underwent several reconstructions at the beginning of the 20th century. It was destroyed in a terrorist attack by the ultra-leftist military wing of the Bulgarian Communist Party in 1925. The act of violence was the biggest of its time and is still the deadliest terrorist attack in Bulgarian history. The church was rebuilt in 1933 with a central dome that hovers 31 metres above the 30 × 15.5 metre nave. The architecture is a belated expression of National Romanticism with Byzantine-influenced elements. It could be viewed as a local analogue of the rationalised European classicism of the time. The external walls are clad in bigor, a local type of travertine, which is also used in neighbouring buildings, in particular the Seat of the Bishop of Sofia, on the opposite side of the square. The eight bells were donated by the Russian governor, Prince Dondukov-Korsakov in 1879. The Bulgarian Exarch Joseph I and the Bishop of Sofia Parteny are buried inside the church.

Unicredit Bulbank (former Bulgarian Foreign Trade Bank)

018
CC

7 Sveta Nedelya Square
Vladimir Romenski,
Kremena Romenska
1992

The building is located right next to the antique Forum of Serdica. Its silhouette is an attempt to reinterpret the lost outline of the urban block. The entrance space is carved into the building as part of a covered piazza, forming a semi-public pedestrian space. The massive top floor and the glazed vertical communications alongside the boulevard are the guiding motifs of the design. The bank was conceived as an additional component of the landmark ensemble of buildings on the square and a replica of the monumental buildings from the 1950s to the east of it. The construction is based on a 20-metre quadratic grid to allow flexibility and a minimal number of supports, because of still-to-be-unearthed archaeological remains. The small balcony on the front refers to that of the National Bank.

Largo Square Ensemble

019

CC

1 Knyaz Dondukov Blvd/
Knyaginya Maria Luiza Blvd
Kosta Nikolov and team
1956

The ensemble of buildings on Largo Square is the largest such group in the city and formed as the centre of political power. It was built in the 1950s on traces of the Decumanus Maximus of Ancient Serdica, underneath the city level. The architecture of the three massive buildings, which surround the square, is a Stalinist reading of Roman grandeur. On the north side is the Council of Ministers, linked to the Central Universal Store, a shopping centre said to be the largest of its era in the Balkans. On the south is the Presidency with the Sheraton Hotel next to it. The building at the centre of the symmetrical composition initially housed the Bulgarian Communist Party, and is still called Party House. Opposite this was a vast statue of Lenin, which has today been replaced. The concept of the entire complex was to demonstrate the power and sturdiness of the totalitarian State. Each of the three buildings surrounds an inner courtyard. Though symmetrical, the two side buildings have slight differences, such as the neo-Romanesque arcades on the northern one. Both entrances project outwards and end with triangular frontispieces – the one above the Council of Ministers features two figures representing labour (by D. Dimitrov, B. Tilov). The interior of the foyer of the Council is designed in neo-Byzantine and National Romantic styles, reflecting the architectural language of the beginning of the 20th century. The quiet courtyard of the President's Office frames the well-preserved St George Church (see 034), an ancient rotunda that springs out of the remains of the Roman city. The southern part of the complex, designed predominantly by Dimitar Tsolov

and his team, stretches out to Saborna Street, and has its strong presence on Sveta Nedelya Square, with the central entrance of the Sheraton Hotel. Party House was designed by Petar Zlatev and team, under consultation with Dimitar Tsolov and the Russian B. Blokhin. Its front façade gradually narrows in height from the entrance portico up to the thick spire, which once supported a star made of ruby glass (see 240). Party House was supposed to stand directly opposite the House of the Soviets, an unrealised building designed as an almost-100-metre-high culmination of the complex to the west. Since 2011, Party House has accommodated the Parliament offices. Though the building's central position seems to correlate to the importance of the institution, its overall appearance has not changed, and so its political connotations remain. In recent years, several architectural competitions have been announced to realise the idea of moving Parliament's Plenary Hall into the former Party House – a rather controversial yet persistent idea. In 2016 a new sky-lit public space was created at the archaeological level (see 020).

НАРОДНО СЪБРАНИЕ

Glass domes over archaeological remains

020
CC

1 Nezavisimost Square
Hristo Guentchev Jr., Johannes Baar-Baarenfels
2016

Under Nezavisimost (or Independence) Square lie the ruins of the Roman city of Serdica. During the works for the Sofia metro, this Roman layer, 6–7 metres under ground level, was partially restored and shown in a new space conceived as a multifunctional hall. It was then covered by three flat glass domes with a maximum height of 2.1 metres, so as not to block the views to the square. The domes are located so that there is enough space to walk between them. They have a double-curved geometry, made from a steel structure covered with glass panels. Though the skylights are rather flat, their presence radically changed the appearance of the square. These 'reflective bubbles' have brought a kind of futuristic, surreal quality to the surrounding Stalinist buildings, converting the location into the mise-en-scène of an anti-utopian film.

View towards Largo Square and the building complex containing the Presidency and the Sheraton Hotel

Two apartment buildings ↑↓
021
CC
5 and 7 Knyaz Dondukov Boulevard
Georgi Ganev
1956

These two residential buildings were designed and constructed along with Party House, the former headquarters of the Bulgarian Communist Party (BCP). The apartments were determined for the administrative staff of the BCP's Central Committee and therefore open luxuriousness was not an aim. The design is austere and strongly geometric, with restricted decoration and moderate expressiveness. Both edifices may be regarded as informative stylistic samples and create the impression that they have come out of the pages of a Soviet architectural magazine of the time. A typical stylistic change compared to the previous modernist trend is the shaping of the corners. While in the modernist and art deco traditions corners were treated as space-defining nodes, in the buildings of the Stalinist era, they were much heavier and clad in rusticated stone. Both façades share a similar classicistic tripartite composition. The double pilasters in the attics lend some lightness to the otherwise stubborn façades

Administration building for the Sofia Municipality (current GIS offices) →
022
CC
5 Serdica Sreet
Konstantin Dzhangozov
1937

The building is one of the earliest projects by Konstantin Dzhangozov, who graduated in Paris in 1934 and shortly afterwards was commissioned to design an office building for the Sofia Municipality. Originally three floors high, the edifice was upgraded with two additional levels in the years after the Second World War. The convex curve of the corner flows in full harmony with the horizontal window strips. The ground floor is fully glazed and set back behind a colonnade, which, along with the whiteness of the limestone-clad upper floors, creates a harsh distinction between the upper and lower parts of the building. That separation and the bands of windows are apparent references to the five principles of Le Corbusier. At the same time, Dzhangozov designed the new chimney of the nearby Mineral Bathhouse. Though this office building was a purely utilitarian object, its design represents the modernist ideas of the time.

Administrative building (formerly Bulgarian Phoenix insurance company offices) →

023

CC

21 Knyaz Dondukov Boulevard
Georgi Fingov, Dimo Nichev, Georgi Yurukov
1927

Set at the beginning of a central boulevard, this building sets the scale for future developments. Air raids during the Second World War destroyed the baroque roof and severely damaged the sculpture of a phoenix atop of the remarkable clock. The symmetry of the façades is accentuated by the central elements above the ground floor: slim Ionic pilasters with protruding balconies in between. These lead up to is a one-storey pediment with arched windows. Two eagle sculptures guard the entrance. The interior is opulently covered in travertine, marble, polished granite, and wood panelling. The architecture is an original expression of European neo-historicism.

Ikoniyska. The name 'Samardzhiyska' was added later as a reference to the neighbouring quarter of the saddle craftsmen (*samardzhii*). The church is a small single-nave building. The picturesque texture of the walls, made up of mixed masonry with antique spolio (recycled stone fragments), river stones of different colours, and brick rows, enhance the urban and artistic qualities of the small volume. The church was preserved in the course of the realisation of an underground passway at the beginning of the 1960s and later restored. Some wall-painting fragments from the 14th, 15th, and 16th centuries remain in the interior.

St Petka Samardzhiyska Church 024

CC

Nezavisimost Square
Restoration: Nikola Mushanov, Zlatka Kirova, Lubomir Delchev
11th century, 14th–16th century (wall paintings), 16th century (St Pimen Zografski Cloister), 1978 (restoration)

The church was built in the 11th century on a site with a long history as a sacred place. On the underground level is a preserved crypt from the 4th century. The remains of Roman tombs reveal that there was an older cult building in the same place. In the 3rd–4th centuries, the church was dedicated to St Petka

Banya Bashi Mosque ↓→ 025

CC

Banski Square/Knyaginya Maria Luiza Boulevard
Attributed to Mimar Sinan.
Reconstruction and restoration: Hristo Ganchev, Lazar Mishev
mid-16th century, 1983 (restoration)

The construction of the mosque was financed by Molla Effendi Kadi Seifullah, so it is therefore also known as 'Molla Effendi' or 'Kadi Seifullah'. Some sources site the Ottoman architect Mimar Sinan, famous in the times of Sultan Suleiman I the Magnificent, as the author of the edifice. The mosque is an example of the

single-domed mosque type with a quadrangle plan, inspired by the Roman and Byzantine traditions. This type was widespread in the Ottoman Empire from the 14th century onwards and also in the Balkans from the 15th and 16th centuries. The dome, with its diameter of 15 metres, rests upon eight segments, supported by a mixed structure of four squinches and eight pendentives. The pendentives are located under the dome, between the wall arches and the trompe arches. Pairs of flying buttresses support the dome on the outside. The Ottoman traveller Evliya Çhelebi (1611–1682), who vividly described his journeys, wrote: 'The minaret is very beautiful and there is no other like this one in Sofia.' The sculptural decoration on the minaret's balcony is another conspicuous feature of the house of worship.

National Bank of Bulgaria (BNB) ensemble

026
CC

1 Knyaz Alexander I Battenberg Square and Atanas Burov Square
National Bank of Bulgaria (BNB): *Dimitar Tsolov, Ivan Vasilyov, Hristo Peshev, Boris Kapitanov. Stained glass: Dechko Uzunov, Ivan Penkov. Sculpture: Lubomir Dalchev, Mihaylo Paraschuk. Stained glass in renovation: Marin Marinov*
1939, 2006 (renovation)
National Archaeological Museum (former Buyuk Mosque/Ul Mosque; now Grand Vizier Mahmud Pasha Mosque): 1451–1494

The ensemble of the National Bank and the National Archaeological Museum integrates the inherited building of the National Museum, sheltered in the former mosque since 1892. The mosque is the oldest preserved Islamic religious building in Sofia. It belongs to the Anatolian typology of the multi-cellular (multi-domed or Seljuk-style) mosques, created in the second half of the 14th century. It is thought that the architect Ayvaz Pasha is the author of the archetype for these mosques, which later spread throughout the entire Balkan region. Four columns form the space, which is subdivided into nine quadratic modules. These sections are covered with domes set on octagonal tympanums

and pendentives. The exceptions are the domes of the central nave, which are set on triangular-shaped squinches. The three central-nave domes are higher and thus direct the mosque's composition from the entrance in the north-west, to the mihrab, and towards Mecca to the south-east. A two-storey anteroom was added to the north-western front, in 1905, to organise the main entrance and the administration of the museum. In the course of the construction of the National Bank, the museum was extended southwards. Through its abstract and simplified classicist language with elements of rationalism, the bank building represents the stability of the institution. Its interior is organised around the monumental space of the central hall, which recalls a courtyard or public square. The synthesis of the stylised neoclassical architecture with the decorative and fine arts defines the bank interior as a late and simplified example of art deco. The small balcony above the figure of St Nikola makes a stylistic connection to the mosque. The architecture of the mosque, the new wings, and the bank building form contextual links that are unique in Bulgarian architecture. The transition of the front's shape, from the medieval cell-brickwork to the rationalised Byzantine style and the modernised classicist elevations, is enhanced by the change in the colours of the materials.

Central State Archives (former Assicurazioni Generali & Vitosha insurance company)
027
CC
5 Moskovska Street
Assen Mihaylowski
ca. 1939

The building is located in a square and its impact comes through its clear and modernist main façade. It accommodates shops on the ground floor, a café on the first floor, offices on the upper levels, and a restaurant with terrace on the top floor. The detail-free façade, the flat roof, and the lack of window frames complete the rationalist look. The horizontal rows of uniform windows emphasise the slight curvature of the façade, whose solid plane hovers above the glazed ground floor and is topped by an airy pergola. The bay window on the first level acts as a counterpoint to the slope of the terrain and signifies the edge of the building, adding dynamism to the composition. Because of changes in the street level, the ground floor was reconstructed and new stairs were added.

Office building (former Karadzhata Apartments) ↗
028
CC
3 Moskovska Street
Petar Karasimeonov, Krastan Getchev
1929

Once the northern front of Alexander I Square, this building today stands in the shadow of Party House. It consisted of shops on the ground floor and apartments on the upper levels. The composition is determined by the frontal perception on the one hand, and the presence of the small street which requires an asymmetrical design solution on the other. The pure modernist façade is well balanced. The horizontal bands of windows could still be read, though after the reconstruction, the dark wall spans between them were clad in the same white limestone as the rest of the façade. The background is formed by the uniform order of the windows. Small balconies emphasise the horizontality and the corner. Their solid parapets replaced the previous metal railings.

Nikolay Binev Youth Theatre and offices (former hotel and Balkan Cinema) ↓ 029 CC

8–10 Knyaz Dondukov Boulevard
Stancho Belkovski, Ivan Danchov. Reconstruction: Russi Tabakov
1937, 1945 and 2006 (reconstruction)

This building accommodates the theatre foyer and some shops on the ground floor, while the offices are on the mezzanine level. The upper floors were once a hotel made up of apartments, but have now been converted into offices. The architecture refrains from subdividing the compact volume into parts. The repetition of the apartment motif in the elevation (a window with a small loggia) gives the building a unified and densely-packed air. The elevations are free of sculptural motifs and decoration, and finish abruptly in the eaves. The initial design of the cinema was altered for the needs of the theatre in the course of its reconstructions, one in 1945 and another in 2006. The building is an example of the rational functionalism seen in architecture of the 1930s.

Ministry of Defence ↓ 030 CC

3 Dyakon Ignatiy Street
Adolf Václav Kolář. Reconstruction: Ivan Vasiliov, Dimitar Tsolov. Sculptures: Lyuben Dimitrov, Mihailo Parashchuk. Stained glass: Georgi Atanasov
1885, 1939 (stained glass), 1945 (reconstruction)

The Ministry was constructed in a neo-Renaissance style. It is an important element of the architectural framework of the City Garden. The building was initially two storeys high with a corner tower on three levels, decorated with a balustrade. Both wings ended with risallites of classical frontons on monumental colonnades. Another colonnade with an attic enhanced the visibility of the entrance. From 1939 to 1945, the building was completely rebuilt and altered. The new edifice was designed in the spirit of a reduced neoclassicism. The grand colonnade gives the building a ceremonious image. Reliefs and masks of Bulgarian kings decorate the elevation. The interiors are noteworthy, especially the stained-glass windows in the staircase and the wooden carvings in the conference hall.

BACB bank building (former Chamber of Commerce and Industry) ↑

031

CC

2 Slavyanska Street
Georgi Fingov, Dimo Nichev, Nikola Jurukov; 1915

The rounded tower is well exposed on a street corner and forms an unified ensemble with the surrounding property. The architecture of the edifice is a variation on the neo-baroque style, with arched windows, balconies, plaster ornaments, and other elements such as balusters and cartouches.

Union of Bulgarian Composers ↓

032

CC

2 Ivan Vazov Street
Milko Pindev
1961

This angular structure is situated in an environment dominated by the richly decorated and brightly coloured neo-baroque architecture of the Ivan Vazov National Theatre, and the Gendovich and Vatev apartment buildings that shape the nearby corners. Milko Pindev created a free and artistic combination of typical, yet individually designed motifs from a modernist vocabulary, to enter into a dialogue with the neo-historical neighbourhood. The building seems to hover above its high colonnade and its transparent parterre. The joints of the stone-covered panels that clothe the façade form a horizontal pattern, a continuation of the main raster. A well-proportioned roof-pergola completes the façade. The building contains offices, meeting rooms, and a concert hall. A bookshop, initially located on the ground-floor parterre, was moved to a small pavilion outside the building. The edifice is the odd one out among its ornate neighbours: its orthogonal grid of straight lines sits in sharp contrast to the soft edges of the ornamentation on the surrounding structures. As the building is also set back from the others, it garners still more attention.

Hristo Gendovich's house
5 Dyakon Ignatiy Street
Nikola Lazarov
1914

033
CC

The building is placed on a corner and forms part of the public square in front of the National Theatre. Initially an apartment block, it consists of a ground level, a mezzanine, and four storeys. The architect created variations on themes from the French eclectic school of the late 19th century. The shape is defined by the three-storey oriels and the vertical rhythm of the balconies in between, and to some extent resembles the silhouette of a vernacular house. The ground level elevation was reorganised and so lost its original decorative and artistic value.

St George Rotunda

034

CC

2a Knyaz Dondukov Boulevard
Restoration and reconstruction: Damian Damianov, Stoyan Yanev. Wall Paintings: Liuba Krasovska;
4th century, 1977 (restoration)

The rotunda was probably part of the Roman Forum complex situated to the west of it, facing the Cardo Maximus. The remains of the Bouleuterion located on the Cardo Maximus have been documented, but no longer exist. The rotunda is the only relatively well-preserved Roman public building from the beginning of the 4th century. Its symmetrical space is composed of four orthogonal cross-axes. The main access to it is along an east–west axis from the entrance to the central domed space. This space dominates the composition of the building. Its ground plan is typical for the Roman cult buildings of the period in their Middle East variants: an eight-sector symmetry with four conches around a cupola of 9.75 metres in diameter. The dome, with a height of 14 metres, was destroyed during Late Antiquity. Its general features define the building as a Martyrium or a Baptisterium from the early days of Christianity in Bulgaria. In the 15th century the rotunda was used as a Bulgarian metropolitan church. At the beginning of the 16th century it was converted into a mosque, known as the Gul Djamy ('Rose Mosque'). After the National Liberation from the Ottoman Empire, the rotunda served as a mausoleum for the remains of the first Bulgarian prince Alexander I Battenberg from 1893 to 1898. In the north-west conche was an antique fragment with floral motifs from 4th–6th centuries. The three strata of medieval paintings from the 10th, 12th, and 14th centuries are the most important artistic pieces in the building. The 10th-century wall paintings enclose the frieze between the windows and the dome's base. In the northern part there are fragments of images of flying angels, one of which is of special interest. Sixteen prophet figures are depicted between the window openings. Below them, in a belt between the windows and the base of the arches, are 12th-century paintings of 12 prophets. Gospel scenes and the four evangelists are represented on the other walls and in the half-domed parts of the conches. A layer of paintings from the 14th century forms a stripe consisting of two sections: the central medallion with the figure of Jesus Christ surrounded by four flying angels and the four evangelists; and underneath is a frieze showing 22 prophets. The St George Rotunda is a listed monument of national importance.

Gladstone apartment building
27 William Gladstone Street
Vasko Vassilev
1943

035
CC

Some apartment buildings of the late 1930s and early 1940s, such as this one, constructed from 1939 to 1943, present the freshest ideas of the International Style in combination with fine neoclassical elements. The apartment buildings by Vasko Vassilev are recognisable through their curved windows, expressive convex volumes, and single recessed top floors. Vassilev's delicate blending of the two styles is seen in the symmetrical composition with limestone cladding and the cast-iron railings in the cut-outs on the parapets. He also designed the interior spaces of the building visible on the ceiling of the passageway to the inner courtyard.

SofBuild offices

036

CC

7–9 Uzundzhovska Street
LT Consult, Atanas Panov, Lorita Panova, Maria Tzekova, Ivaylo Kastrev, Iskren Manev
2003

This five-floor office building is located in the central part of the city, on a small street next to Vitosha Boulevard, a lively pedestrian thoroughfare. It is an infill set close to a building on the one side, and with a blind wall to a neoclassicist house on the other side. The new glass volume connects to the old house by continuing its cornice. The cornice gradually protrudes as it reaches the corner, orienting the building towards the boulevard. On the other side, it turns into a solid wall, treated in the same way as the roof. One minimal architectural gesture solved all of the conflicts and satisfied the requirements. The building was nominated for the 2005 Mies van der Rohe Award.

Apartment building
39 Solunska Street
Neno Yamantiev
1953

037
CC

Conceived in a period dominated by the norm 'national in form, socialist in content' – an official concept that often resulted in a Classical composition with some vernacular propaganda as decoration – this building has a much deeper significance. The façade composition develops on several different levels. At first glance, it seems to be divided into three parts. On the ground floor, the shops form a rigid base. The middle part has a Classical development – the colossal order, in front of the recessed façade. The upper part contains aspects of Bulgarian vernacular renaissance architecture – the wavy cornice and the glazing over it. The colossal-order columns feature inversed convex cannelures. However, the ease with which all of these elements are combined, the use of Classical detail in a free, sometimes ironic manner, and the various references – Classical, vernacular, and even modernist – all create a singular image.

Office building (former Imperial Hotel)

038

CC

2a Saborna Street

Kiril Marichkov

1920

At the time of its erection, the Imperial Hotel was the most luxurious in Bulgaria. It welcomed many prominent visitors, among them members of the Japanese royal family. The emblematic architecture is a late expression of the eclecticism of the second half of the 19th century. The imposing neo-baroque building was crowned with a double mansard roof and a domed corner tower, some Secessionist details, and an interior in the spirit of the Biedermeier style. The building was damaged in the air raids during the Second World War, but thanks to its architectural shape and quality, it was incorporated into the new governmental centre in the early 1950s. Some functional changes have reflected negatively upon the architectural integrity of the interior. Recently, the structure and the proportions of the wall openings on the ground floor and the mezzanine were radically changed. The building is an important landmark and towers over the corner near the City Garden.

Chief Mufti's Office

039

CC

27 Bratya Miladinovi Street/ Stefan Stambolov Boulevard

Naum Torbov

1909

This is a rare example of residential architecture from the beginning of the 20th century. It is well exposed on a sharp corner and integrates organically into the urban structure. The building was initially a private house belonging to Dimitar and Louisa Stanishev, with shops on the ground floor. Later it housed public institutions. Today it is used as the Chief Mufti's Office. The most interesting artistic element is the corner, which is flanked by two curved tower-oriels with neo-baroque cupolas. The tower motifs recall romanticist castles of the 19th century. The side elevations are finished by semicircular eaves. The building can be classified stylistically as an early Secession interpretation of historic styles. The palm-chapters of the pilasters holding the oriels show an interesting mixture of Eastern and Western influences. Though the building is not an achievement of the highest level, it does represent a local understanding of the philosophical and aesthetic roots of the Secession.

Bank building (former Bulgarian National Bank) ↑

040 CC

12 Prince Alexander I Street
Jacob Heinrich Meier.
Decoration: Marin Vasilev.
Superstructure: Nikola Zankov.
Reconstruction: Boris Kapitanov
1895 (decoration), 1919 (superstructure), 1960 (reconstruction)

This neo-baroque building is part of the continuous architectural frame of the City Garden. The initial building was extended with a two-storey superstructure in 1919. The symmetry on the front is underlined by a risalit, framed by two large-scale pilasters with a secondary attic and a rectangular dome above. The same order of flat pilasters, rustically treated on the ground floor, runs along both elevations. The two-figure sculpture is an important document of the artistic debate in the post-Liberation period and Bulgarian society's strong inclination towards European culture.

Office building ↗ (former French-Belgian Bank)

041 CC

17 Lege Street
Georgi Fingov, Dimo Nichev, Georgi Yurukov; 1925

The street-facing front of this building has a monumental look, with aspects such as the arched and rectangular windows, the intricate balustrade and cornices, and the pilasters and half-columns that run along two floors. The artistic appearance is completed by the sculpted frames of the second-floor windows, the stone fragments, and the three large reliefs depicting symbols of trade. The bank hall in the centre of the building and the hall gallery are both lit by skylights. The architecture is an example of the late neoclassicist trend developed in the interwar period. In 1986 a heavy mansard floor was added, violating the building's proportions.

Telephone and Telegraph Hall ↑ 042 CC

2–4 General Gurko Street
Stancho Belkovski
1947

Designed before the Second World War, the Telegraph and Telephone Hall possesses the characteristics of monumental classicism in the style's simplified 'minimalist' variant. Its monumental appearance is strengthened by the raised ground-floor level and the enormous open stairs leading up to the main entrance. The light-coloured front façade is decorated with heraldic stone reliefs.

Central Post Office ↓ 043 CC

General Gurko Street/
Dyakon Ignatiy Street
Yordan Milanov.
Reconstruction: Assen Mihaylovski, Vladimir Brankov
1893, 1940 (reconstruction)

This huge edifice occupies an entire urban block and was designed in the spirit of interwar modernised classicism, with two symmetrically protruding volumes. A prominent cornice divides the attic from the rest of the building. The original design from the 19th century has been preserved in one of the halls.

View towards the City Garden, with part of the Bulgarian National Bank (040) and the cupolas of the National Archaeological Museum (former Buyuk Mosque; 026)

National Art Gallery (former Princely and Royal Palace)

044

CC

1 Knyaz Alexander I Square
Viktor Rumpelmayer, Jakob Heinrich Meyer, Adolf Václav Kolář, Leers. Friedrich Grünanger, Franz Aysler, Yanaki Shamardzhiev. Wall paintings and stained-glass windows: Anton Mitov, Ivan Murkvichka. Stefan Badzhov. Reconstruction: Yordan Sevov, Ivan Vasilyov.
1883, 1895, 1897 (wall paintings, stained glass), 1926, ca. 1930 (reconstruction)

The building was erected as the Seat of the Ottoman administration and as the headquarters of the district governor. After National Liberation, the building was adapted to the needs of the re-established Bulgarian State as a residence of Prince Alexander I Battenberg, in 1883. It was then enlarged to the north, and designed in Viennese neo-baroque style. The baroque staircase in the central axis of the building is the core of its enfilade spatial composition. The administration rooms were linked to the main entrance by two side corridors. The complex was completed by an imposing baroque fence. The first construction phase involved the realisation of the Palace Court and the City Garden. The latter was designed as a public space adjacent to the palace complex. The second

© Plamen Agov • studiolemontree.com

construction phase took place in 1895, during the reign of Prince Ferdinand. A new residential tract was added to the north-east side and the artistic decoration of the interior was enriched. In 1928, at the eastern end of the complex, the Natural Science Museum, was erected to complete the street front. After the Second World War, the palace was used as the Seat of the Council of Ministers. To create Knyaz Alexander I Square as it is today, the level of the Palace Court was lowered by 2 metres. In the 1960s, the palace building was converted into the National Art Gallery, to house its collection of the valuable artworks from both Bulgaria and abroad.

BNP Paribas bank building (former Sofia Club House) ↓

045
CC

2 Tsar Osvoboditel Boulevard
Peter Paul Brang.
Restoration, reconstruction, and superstructure: Georgi Kolarov
1890, 2001 (restoration)

During reconstructions in 2001, the classicist façades of this former club house were restored, and a two-storey superstructure was added. The ground-level arcade at was also rehabilitated, and the later addition of an attic was removed. The integrity and contrast between the old and new architecture was attained by a double-mansard roof made of glass.

Rakovski/Graf Ignatiev Street apartment building →

046
CC

149 Georgi Sava Rakovski Street
Hristo Berberov
1937

The use of glass for whole building-volumes or even just façades was strongly influenced by the Bauhaus building in Dessau, Germany (Walter Gropius, 1925). Although no Bulgarian architects graduated from the Bauhaus vocational school in the building, the concept of glass façades spread. One of the best examples in Sofia is this apartment block designed by Hristo Berberov in 1937. The rationality of the main façade is achieved by the uniform rhythm of the windows and by the joints in the flush limestone cladding. The glass-enclosed cantilevered volume, with its expressive triangular plan, stands as a counterpoint to the rigid composition. The horizontal grid and the thin metal frames of the glass volume enclose the conservatories. The motif of a triangular cantilever, which adds dynamism to this edifice, can be seen in another apartment building by the same architect on Garibaldi Square (see 057). With its recessed rooftop terrace, the upper part of the building also follows the Corbusian spirit of Modern Movement architecture.

Federation of Scientific and Technical Unions (former Bulgarian Architectural and Engineering Society) ↘

047
CC

108 Georgi Sava Rakovski Street
Todor Goranov, Boris Rusev.
Bas-relief: Hristo Haralampiev
1930, 2003 (bas-relief)

The building is an infill in an urban block. It was initially constructed as the headquarters of the Bulgarian Architectural and Engineering Society and therefore has a conference hall suitable for movie shows, other cultural performances, and exhibitions. After the Second World War the building was adapted to the requirements of the Federation of Scientific and Technical Unions. In terms of style, the architecture is a mixture of late neoclassicism with baroque elements and ornaments.

The façade is dominated by four columns, set in front of the three floors in the middle of the classical body. The columns headed by Ionian capitals have console modillions at the mezzanine level. The rustically plastered surfaces on the ground and mezzanine floors and on the side walls above the classical base frame the column order in the central part of the edifice.

City Garden (former Alexandrovska Garden, dedicated to the Emperor Alexander II and the Popular Garden) →

048
CC

Knyaz Alexander I Battenberg Square/Dyakon Ignatiy Street/General Joseph Gurko Street/Knyaz Alexander I Battenberg Street
Adolf Václav Kolář, Karl Bets, Daniel Neff. Atanas Agura. Fountain: Georgi Chapkanov
1878, 1976 (fountain)

Information about the planted area dates back to 1837. The decision to organise a fenced public garden was taken in 1869. A central composition of two axes and a circular alley was formed in 1887. The garden was initially connected with the Royal Palace in a joined green system and was limited in the south-west by

Saborna Street. The extension to the contemporary configuration was carried out in 1895, when the north-eastern part was added to the Palace, and separated by Tsar Osvoboditel Boulevard. As a result, the composition received two centres with picturesque patterns. The cross-axis from Ivan Vazov Street was duplicated by the continuation of Slavyanska Street at the beginning of the 20th century, and a longitudinal axis from the Palace to General Joseph Gurko Street was created. The geometric, classicist composition changed between the wars to a picturesque, romanticist one, but the link between the City Garden and the Palace Garden was preserved. The two gardens appeared as a united green area in the macro structure of the city, until in 1947 the square was set between them. That integrity was completely reorganised by the erection of the Mausoleum of Georgi Dimitrov on the north-eastern edge of the City Garden, directly opposite the palace (Georgi Ovcharov, Racho Ribarov, Ivan Danchov, 1949; mosaics: Dechko Uzunov, 1975). The longitudinal axis was redesigned with a touch of classicism in the 1950s, while the periphery preserved its romanticist patterns (seen in the photo above). A reconstruction was carried out in 1976, when a water pool with fountains and a sculpture were constructed at the cross-point of the main axes. After the fall of Communism in 1999, the Mausoleum was demolished. A number of elements corresponding to the development phases can be observed today, but they do not express an integral space concept of the previously united composition of the two parks. Nevertheless, the principal elements of its frame still exist.

Hotel Rila ↓
6 Tsar Kaloyan Street
Georgi Stoilov
1962

049
CC

This building marked the first phase of new hotel design in the spirit of modernism. An administrative reform carried out in 1959 demanded that every central city in Bulgaria's 29 districts have a hotel for business and tourism. Hotel Rila is located in the heart of the historic centre of Sofia. Its structure consists of two volumes: a lower public one and the hotel part 'hovering' above it. These parts are separated by a recessed storey. The loggias – typical elements of holiday architecture, though not common in urban hotels – are legitimated by the remarkable view towards Vitosha Mountain from the upper storeys and the view onto the small garden in front of the hotel.

Ivan Vazov National Theatre
Dyakon Ignatiy Street
Ferdinand Fellner, Hermann Helmer. Martin Duelfer. Ivan Tomov, Lilia Toteva, Zlatka Kojuharova (artist)
1906, 1928, 1976

050
CC

The spot has served as a theatre since 1888 when the first wooden building was erected there. Just over a decade later, in 1899, the Municipality of Sofia commissioned the project for a new theatre to the Viennese architecture practice Fellner & Helmer. Their building faces the side of the City Garden, with a piazza in front of it and the fountains at its axis. The entrance is a monumental portico set upon a pediment. The side towers are crowned by sculptures by Ernst Hegenbarth. The interior design was the work of Friedich Voelkl, Bothe & Ehrmann, and Joseph Schmied, the author of the stucco paintings. The murals in the auditorium were painted by Rudolf Fuchs. After a fire in 1923, the Bulgarian National Theatre was reestablished with the idea to reconstruct and enlarge the building. The design by the German architect Martin Duelfer, appointed for the project after a competition, changed the initial proportions of the building enormously. The general integrity of the edifice was recovered after the restoration of the initial concept, which took place from 1972 to 1976.

Ivan Vazov National Theatre from above

050

Hotel complex and Bulgaria Concert Hall

051

CC

4 Tsar Osvoboditel Boulevard,
1 Aksakov Street
Stancho Belkovski, Ivan Danchov
1937

The construction of this complex was commissioned by the Clerical Cooperative Savings and Insurance Company. The competition was launched in 1931, construction began in spring 1935, and the complex opened in October 1937. Over a total area of 4,200 square metres the complex had a mixed programme for a hotel, a restaurant, a cafe, a beer hall, rooms for receptions and celebrations, a summer and a winter garden, and a large concert hall with adjacent service spaces. With its marvellous expressionist staircase, the

restaurant area was one of the most imposing in Sofia at the time. It was also equipped with a sliding roof, which transforms the interior space into an open courtyard. The concert hall, initially meant for 1,470 visitors, was destroyed during the Second World War, along with its organ made by Wilhelm Sauer. The hall was re-erected in 1949. A Schuke organ was installed in 1974. The concert hall is home to the Sofia Philharmonic Orchestra, Bulgaria's first professional symphony orchestra, established in 1928, and has become an emblematic place for classical music in the city. The directness of the interior design and the transitions of the interior elements and spaces create an integrity, despite the building's diverse functions. These characteristics classify the complex as Streamline Moderne with expressionist elements.

European Parliament and European Commission administrative building

052

CC

Georgi Sava Rakovski Street/
Racho Dimchev Street
ProArch/Maya Yovcheva
2008

The building was initially designed as a mixed-use retail space, but was later chosen for the headquarters of the European Parliament and the European Commission in Bulgaria. The entire internal layout was changed according to the new requirements. The first three levels above the ground floor are organised as exhibition areas and presentation halls, with free access from the corner of Georgi Sava Rakovski Street. The other levels are used as offices for the European Parliament and European Commission, with restricted access. The cafeteria on the top floor provides magnificent views across the rooftops of Sofia. The shape of the metal-and-glass building recalls a uniform crystalline structure. The contrast between the new office building and older residential ones is enhanced by its corner position on a busy street that passes some of Sofia's main landmarks.

View towards the Ministry of Internal Affairs (053) and St Sedmochislenitsi Church (former Mosque Kodzha Dervish Mehmed Pasha; 054)

054

Ministry of Internal Affairs

053

CC

29 6th September Street
Georgi Ovcharov. Lion sculpture: Mihail Mihaylov, Georgi Ovcharov
1940

The design was the winning entry in a competition for the Ministry of Internal Affairs offices in 1936. The U-shaped building occupies the western part of an urban block. The northern face is one storey higher and makes a gentle curve along General Joseph Gurko Street in order to widen the pedestrian space at the corner, and to come at a right angle to the western elevation. Its length is stressed by a low stone-clad wall, which visually separates the pavement from the semi-public space along the building, ending with a lion sculpture. The elevation design is sober and minimalist to underline the solidity of the building volumes. Despite its monumental expression, the building clearly radiates an air of Romantic vision, typical for the work of Georgi Ovcharov. The project lives at the cross-section between rationalist classicism and expressionist dynamics. This hybrid language can also be seen in the design and furniture in its interior spaces.

St Sedmochislenitsi Church (former Kodzha Dervish Mehmed Pasha Mosque)

054
CC

25 Graf Ignatiev Street
Mimar Sinan. Conversion: Leonid Vasilev. Alexander Pomerantsev, Petko Momchilov, Yordan Milanov
1528, 1898 (conversion), 1903

The ruined 14th-century mosque was adapted to a church by a decree of the Council of Ministers in 1896 and was dedicated to the Bulgarian saints Cyril and Methodius, as well as to their students Kliment, Naum, Sava, Gorazd, and Angelariy. A stone inscription, kept in the National Archaeological Museum, reads: 'The erection of this magnificent, decorated mosque was initiated by the great vizier of Sultan Mehmed-Pasha Tavil ibn Abdul Muzedin in the eighth year (1528) of the reign of the great, tenth-in-line Ottoman Sultan Suleiman the Magnificent.' The dome has a diameter of 18 metres and a height of 22 metres, and it sits upon four squinches. The mosque belongs to the single-dome typology, which has its roots in the Roman and Byzantine empires and developed under the Sasanid Empire. After the conversion, two side porticos and a bell tower were added to the building. The new architecture of the church is a National Romantic interpretation of Byzantine traditions.

Office building (former Union of the Popular Banks and COOP Hotel)

055

CC

Slaveykov Square/
Georgi Sava Rakovski Street
Georgi Ovcharov, Genko Popov
1935

This edifice marks the corner of one of Sofia's liveliest crossroads. The first part of it was built in 1925 along one side of Slaveykov Square. Its shape was further changed in the course of finalising the project in 1935. The mixed-use complex contains hotel rooms, offices, bank halls, shops, and a restaurant. The southern front is slightly curved along Georgi Sava Rakovski Street and ends at a massive corner tower at the junction. The protruding tower with its rectilinear flush walls connects and reconciles the contrasting western and the southern façades. The smooth horizontality of the western elevation is countered by the sharp vertical rhythm of the pilasters on the southern one. That contrast gives a strong expression to the building. Initially, the façades were brick, but soon after the building's construction they were clad in white limestone.

Aleko Konstantinov State Satirical Theatre

056

CC

26 Stefan Karadzha Street
Alexander Dubovik
1948, 1966

The six-storey building with a large hall was built to complement the neighbouring Ministry of Internal Affairs, from 1945 to 1948. It has elements of modernist and late art-deco styles. In the late 1950s and 1960s, after a radical reconstruction, the building was converted into the home of the State Satirical Theatre, named after an eminent Bulgarian writer and satirist.

Apartment building

057

CC

7 Graf Ignatiev Street

Hristo Berberov, Georgi Ovcharov

1935

Situated on an obtuse corner opposite the small Garibaldi Square, this edifice ensures a soft transition between two street fronts. The building connects these fronts at two turns, but the behaviour of the wall system at the turning points seems ambiguous. While the main wall surface curves gently at the corners, parts of it, along with their adjacent windows, continue their straight line, as if by inertia, forming articulated boxes. These sections are sculpturally segregated, creating vertical rhythm and a counterpoint to the soft, floating front. This witty solution provides an organic connection between the modernist building and the surrounding streets – an early manifestation of contextuality in modernist urban architecture. The spaces below the flat roof, now chaotically glazed by the owners, originally formed a large open terrace. The present-day colour of the façade distorts the simplicity and the expressiveness of the concept.

Bulgarian Trade Bank

058

CC

10 Graf Ignatiev Street

Georgi Fingov, Dimo Nichev, Georgi Apostolov

1925

The design for the headquarters of the Bulgarian Trade Bank, also known as the Burov Bros Bank, is one of the most characteristic examples of the blending of art nouveau and art deco in Bulgaria. The sections in these styles were rationalised after the First World War, and some neoclassical overtones were added to the façade. The interior is intricately detailed.

Nedkov and Urumov apartment buildings

059

CC

48 and 59 Vitosha Boulevard
Vasil Radoslavov,
Konstantin Dzhangozov
1939

Symmetrically placed at the corners of Vitosha Boulevard with a secondary street, these two buildings have turned into landmarks for the area. The language of both residential structures uses the whole spectrum of the modernist instrumentarium: strip windows, dynamic balconies, flat roofs, and more. The compact striped façades create dynamic perspectives from the boulevard. The corner balconies play a double artistic role: they follow the elongated appearance of the windows, but at the same time counter the horizontal structure by pulsating back and forth from the front surfaces, thus creating a rhythm of vertical elements. The play of shadows enhances the plastic effect. The curved shape of the corner balconies is completed by the lines of the parterre canopy and the roof terrace, while the corner design of the Urumov building is in contrast rectangular. The corner verticality is underlined by a consolidation of the building

volume on the street side, flanked symmetrically by balconies. The architecture of both buildings is free of any ornamentation since the whole façade articulation plays an ornamental role. The two buildings are in constant dialogue, exchanging variants of modernist typologies across the boulevard span. The relatively large flats are rationally planned. The buildings are exquisite examples of Sofia's pre-war modernism. Both of the building's architects studied in Paris under Auguste Perret (Radoslavov was there at the same time as Le Corbusier), and brought the new expressive systems to Bulgaria.

View towards the park in front of the National Palace of Culture (140) with Patriarch Evtimiy Boulevard to the left

RE/MAX

Centre to East

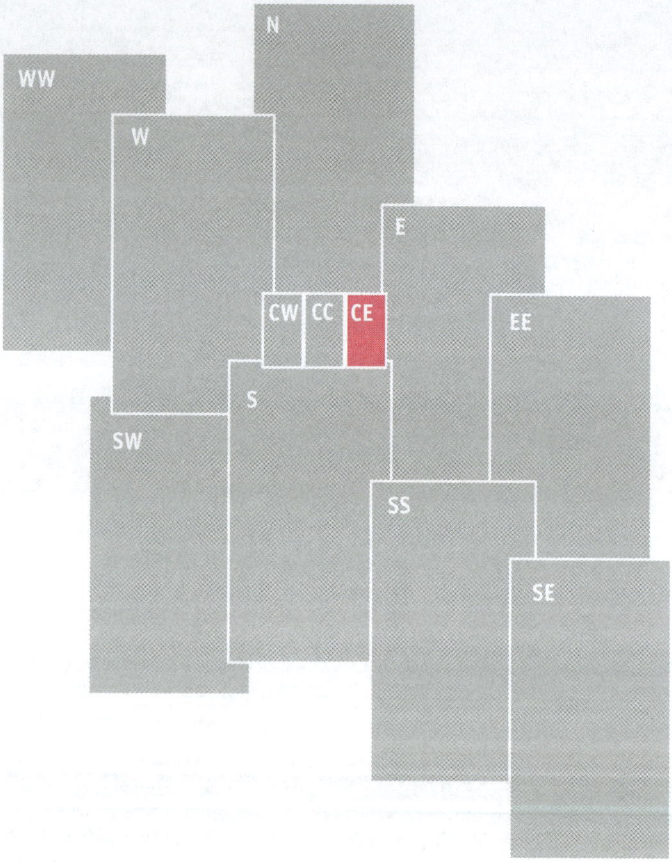

Map CE

The urbanisation of the territory enclosed between the seat of the local governmental officials (now the National Art Gallery) and the Perlovska River began along the road to Istanbul (now Tsar Osvoboditel Boulevard) during Ottoman rule. It was planned and integrated into the urban structure at the end of the 19th century. The religious significance of the sacral hill on which stands the St Alexander Nevski Memorial Cathedral, the topographic conditions, and the radial communication axes all define the public importance and the compositional and social structure of the area. The concentration of religious, governmental, and cultural institutions, as well as the presence of some embassies and a system of green public areas, provoked the interest of many parties, including a number of politicians and businessmen, and led to the erection of high-standard housing quarters in the area. As a result, the territory developed into a well-designed urban area around 1900, and subsequently became a model for the urban renovation of the city. The interventions after the First World War did not change the structure or the social and cultural meaning of the area.

062

St Alexander Nevski Memorial Cathedral (062)

Sacral hill and main necropolis with the Tomb of Honorius ↓

060
CE

Paris Street/Moskovska Street
Restoration: Vassil Kitov.
Design: Mihail Benchev.
Civil engineering: Anton Maleev.
Wall paintings: Vladimir Tsvetkov
4th century CE, 2015 (wall paintings)

A necropolis began to rise outside the city walls at the end of the 2nd century BCE. The typology of the tombs and the different artefacts show that both Christians and non-Christians were buried there – people from different ethnic and social strata. Some remains of churches were found next to the numerous graves. The only completely preserved church is the St Sofia Basilica. The Tomb of Honorius, excavated north-west of the basilica, is an example of the emergence of Christian symbols in the 4th century. This is probably the same Honorius who was a cleric participant of the Council of Serdica in 342 CE. The wall paintings include geometric and floral motifs; large crests with extended ends, each of them decorated with two tassels; and inscriptions in Greek and Latin. The cross points are decorated with medallions with equal-sided open crests. Similar crests can be found in the decoration of the Hagia Sophia in Istanbul and in the mosaics in the Sant' Apollinare in Classe Basilica in Ravenna, both from the 6th century.

St Sofia Church →

061
CE

2 Paris Street
Restoration and reconstruction: Alexander Rashenov. Hristo Ganchev, Damyan Damyanov. Vassil Kitov, Hristo Ganchev. Vassil Kitov, Petar Popov (mosaics)
6th century CE, 1930, 1981, 1999, 2015 (mosaics)

This church, which gave the city its name, was dedicated to the Divine Wisdom Sofia, 'God's Word', or the second face of the Holy Trinity, Jesus Christ. It was built in the 6th century during the reign of Justinian I (483–565) over the remains of three earlier churches. The first building was a single-nave graveyard church with floor mosaics. It was reshaped into a basilica in the 4th century by the addition of two side naves and an apse. The building plan from the 6th century is a combination of two typologies: the Latin-cross space and the Byzantine church with a central dome, both of which emerged in Christian architecture in the last quarter of the 4th century. The arms of the crest along the altar are related to its base, i.e. the length of the nave, with a ratio of 1:3. The central space has a square plan with four corner pillars supporting the dome. The plan of the naos is also square. The ratio the width of the side naves to that of the central one is 3:5. The accuracy of the proportions in the space is unique for

Eastern, as well as Western, church architecture of the time. In the Middle Ages the basilica was a Metropolitan Church. It was used as a mosque during Ottoman rule and abandoned in the 19th century after a series of earthquakes. After Bulgarian Liberation in 1878, the edifice was again converted to a church and was entirely reconstructed from 1930 to 1935. The 'patriarch of Bulgarian literature', writer and poet Ivan Vazov, was buried east of the apse in 1921. A huge Vitosha stone was placed upon his grave, in accordance with his will. The exterior of the church was restored in 1981 to mark the 1,300-year jubilee of the foundation of the Bulgarian State. The same year, the Monument to the Unknown Soldier with its eternal flame (Nikola Nikolov) was erected at the southern side of the church. The core of its composition is a bronze lion created for the site by Andrey Nikolov in 1926. The church's interior was restored in 1999. The unique crypt with exposed Antique graves and the remains of the earlier churches was opened to the public in 2015.

St Alexander Nevski Memorial Cathedral

062

CE

St Alexander Nevski Square

Alexander Pomerantsev, Alexander Jakovlev. Head of construction: Alexander Smirnov. Stone sculpture: Willem Glos, Georgi Kisselinchev. Painters: Alexander Kiselyov, Pyotr Miasoedev, Ivan Murvichka, Nikola Marinov, Tseno Todorov, Haralampi Tachev et al. Bells: P. H. Finnish. Cupola restoration: Veselina Inkova. Glazing: Anton Tornyov. Bells: Paul N. Finnlandski

1912, 2001 (cupola restoration)

The cathedral church of the Patriarch of the Bulgarian Orthodox Church crowns Sofia's sacral hill and is the dominating accent in the urban silhouette. Its location, role, size, and characteristic shape have made it a symbol of the city. The cathedral was dedicated to the Russian prince St Alexander Nevski, saints Cyril and Methodius, and King Boris I. It was erected to commemorate the Liberation and the re-establishing of the Bulgarian State. Construction was funded by donations from ordinary people, and lasted from 1904 to 1912. The cathedral was inaugurated in 1924. It is a five-nave cross-dome building with an imposing area of 3,200 square metres and room for a congregation of about 5,000 people. The architecture is based upon the Eastern Orthodox archetype rooted in Byzantine cross-dome temples from the 6th century. The Byzantine tradition is perceivable in the architectural elements: the bifold and threefold (biphoria and threphoria) subdivision of the windows, chapters, arches, and bows, some metal elements etc. The design was completed with ceramic roof tiles (tegular and imbricate), which were known to have been used in ancient Greek and Thracian constructions and which were also widely used in medieval Byzantine architecture. During construction, the concept was changed, and the roof was covered with gilded copper sheets in the spirit of Russian church architecture. The composition of the wall paintings, mosaics, icons, and wood carvings is subordinate to the overall artistic image and to the idea of synthesis. The cathedral as a whole can be categorised stylistically as a Romantic interpretation in the spirit of the Byzantine cultural sphere, with elements and principles of Russian Classicism and Romanesque architecture.

Synodal Chamber and Patriarchate

063

CE

4 Oborishte Street
Petko Momchilov, Yordan Milanov. Maiolica, ceramics, and mosaics: Haralampi Tachev, Gospodin Zheliazkov
1911

The Synodal Chamber is the seat of the Holy Synod, the supreme authority of the Bulgarian Orthodox Church, and of the Bulgarian Patriarch and Archbishop of Sofia. Its location on the sacral hill, near St Sofia Church, was approved with a decision by the Holy Synod in 1902. The main entrance is an arched portico covered by three domes on eight columns. The building's decoration is a skilful combination of Byzantine medieval traditions and the avant-garde rhetoric of the Secessionist style. In its semantic language one could decode the affiliation of the institution to the local spiritual and cultural context, which was ongoing from the 9th century. The Synod's Chapel is dedicated to Boris I, an Orthodox saint and king who lived during the 9th century. A mosaic on the front elevation shows the leaders in the Bulgarian Orthodox Church's fight for independence (19th century); one of the individuals is Ilarion Makariopolski, the Bishop of Constantinople (Istanbul).

National Opera and House of the Bulgarian Agrarian National Union

064

CE

30 Vrancha Street
Lazar Parashkevanov. Monument of Alexander Stanboliysky: Marko Markov, Stefan Stoimirov. Frieze sculpture: Ilia Petrov, Dechko Uzunov, Ruska Marinova, Stoyo Todorov, Nikola Shmirgela, Ivan Mandov
1954

The design for this building went through various changes in the course of construction. The Bulgarian Agrarian National Union party bought the plot during its short-term in government from 1919 to 1923. The steep terrain was foreseen for the House of the Union containing a congress hall. The initial project from 1922 was in the spirit of modernism. The planning was interrupted after the military putsch against the Union's government in 1923, and was restarted after the Second World War, when the Union ruled together with the Communist Party. The design was remade in classicist style. The Union's diminishing political power led to the separation of the congress hall from the Party rooms and its adaption to the needs of the Opera. Nevertheless, some decoration featuring symbols of the Union, such as the shamrock, were preserved.

National Student House

065

CE

10 National Assembly Square
Stancho Belkovski,
Ivan Danchov
1933

The tradition of student cultural clubs in Bulgaria started in 1901, when the first one was founded. The location was chosen in 1931 and Student House opened in 1933, establishing a centre for the cultural activities of students. A number of creative formations, which left deep traces, were initiated there. As part of the intensive urban development after the First World War, the building holds an important position in contemporary Bulgarian architecture. In the context of the ongoing discussions about the character of Bulgarian architecture, it illustrates the attempt to integrate the aesthetics of the avant-garde into the historical environment. The façade was set back in respect to the mansard roof and the baroque dome of the neighbouring house of Doctor Mollov. The loggia on the top floor and the different shaping of the ground and the upper floors created a plasticity that corresponded to the scale of the surrounding buildings. The horizontal stripes on the elevation predefined the shape of the future architectural frame of the square. Today the building houses ten public studios, offices, four rehearsal halls, an art gallery, and conference halls.

Bank building (former Bulgarian Central Cooperative Bank) ↓

066

CE

1 Ivan Vazov Street
Nikola Lazarov. Extension and superstructure: Georgi Fingov, Dimo Nichev. Dome sculpture: Lyuben Dimitrov
1910, 1930 (dome sculpture)

Initially three storeys tall with a mansard roof, this edifice was later extended with two additional floors. The addition changed the architectural expression of the building from neo-baroque to neo-Renaissance, thus in a strange way reversing the arrow of time. The elevations are decorated with ornaments such as columns, sculptural window frames, and cornices. The corner is marked by a dome, crowned with a sculptural composition of three figures holding the Earth. The building's design shows a strong relationship to European historicism around 1900.

St Nikolay Chudotvorec Russian Church

067

CE

3 Tsar Osvoboditel Boulevard
Alexander Pomerantsev.
Wall Paintings: Vassiliy Perminov, Nikolay Rostovcev. Icons: Mikhail Nesterov. Ivan Jeverjeev, Nikolay Rostovcev. Liturgical Objects: Porphyry Olovianishnikov and sons.
Stone sculpture: Georgi Kisselinchev
1899, 1912 (stone sculpture),
1989 (exterior restoration)

The Russian Church was built for the country's embassy and citizens living in Sofia. It replaced the Saray Mosque, a building that was demolished after the Liberation in 1878. The plot belonged to the embassy, which was situated on the corner of Rakovski and Moskovska streets. The location presupposed the two specific entrances to the church: one from the north – from the garden of the Russian Embassy; and another from the south – from the boulevard for the general public. Thus, the naos space was symbolically converted into a meeting point between two Orthodox Slavic nations. The adjacent plot was later turned into a public garden. The church was named after Nikolay of Myra, the guardian saint of the Russian emperor Nikolay II, who gifted its bells. It is a remarkable document of the Romantic influences of Russian architecture, and could be ranked with early Moscow Baroque buildings from the middle of the 17th century. The silhouette is dominated by five domes covered with golden alloy. That typically Russian volumetric composition stems from the 15th–17th-century vernacular tradition of wooden churches from northern Russia – a tradition that was later revived with baroque features and then transmitted into many Orthodox churches as neo-baroque in the 19th century.

View along Rakovski Boulevard towards Vitosha Mountain

Monument to the King-Liberator Alexander II ↑

068

CE

National Assembly Square
Author: Arnoldo Zocchy.
Architect: Nikola Lazarov.
Restoration: Petar Mitanov, Marin Markov
1907, 2010

The monument dedicated to the Russian emperor Alexander II, who waged the Russian-Turkish Liberation War from 1877 to 1878, features an inscription: 'To the King-Liberator from grateful Bulgaria'. The design was selected in an international competition in 1905 that included architects from more than 10 countries. The monument was inaugurated on 30 August 1907. Some essential changes to the square frame were made throughout the 1930s and 1960s, but the peculiar dialogue between the black-polished-granite emperor on his horse and the National Assembly still continues today. The only preserved building from the time of the erection of the monument is Doctor Mollov's house (architect: Nikola Lazarov), which now serves as an office building.

National Assembly ↙ 069 CE

2 National Assembly Square
Konstantin Jovanovic. Extension: Yordan Milanov. North wing: Pencho Koichev, Alexander Rashenov
1886, 1899 (extension), 1928 (north wing)

The National Assembly (Parliament) was one of the first public buildings erected by the new Bulgarian State. It was symmetrically planned with the plenary hall in its centre. The inscription above the main entrance reads 'United we stand strong'.

Presidium of the Bulgarian Academy of Sciences ↓ 070 CE

1 15th November Street
Jakob Heinrich Meyer. North wing: Yordan Yordanov, Sava Ovcharov
1893, 1928 (north wing)

The building was constructed for the Literary Society, the predecessor of the Bulgarian Academy of Sciences. As there were insufficient funds for construction, members of the Academy took private bank loans for 3 million lev to finish it.

Austrian Embassy (Italian Embassy until 1925) ↑

071

CE

113 Tsar Osvoboditel Boulevard
Enrico Bovio
1910

The edifice was initially used by the Italian Embassy, but came into Austrian ownership after the First World War. The garden in front of it separates the building from the noisy boulevard, while the natural slope in the terrain allowed the building to be positioned higher, which enforced its Classical standing. The design follows a neo-Renaissance language. The curved frontispiece in the axis of symmetry dominates the main elevation and adds to it a pinch of baroque. The mansard roof, the pilasters, the sculptural decorations, and the stone vases all amplify the grand image of the building.

Italian Embassy (Austrian Embassy until 1925)↓

072

CE

111 Tsar Osvoboditel Boulevard
Peter Paul Brang. Reconstruction and extension: Ludwig Richter
1883, 1908 (reconstruction, extension)

The building forms part of a prestigious ensemble on a boulevard created at the end of the 19th century. Its initial design was in a neo-Renaissance spirit and corresponds to that of the Central Military Club (former Sofia Military Officer's Assembly) next to it. The architecture was radically changed in the course of the reconstruction and extension of the building in the 1920s, when it was reshaped in neo-baroque style. The interior includes paintings and furniture from the second half of the 19th century, some of which probably belonged to the Savoy dynasty.

National Academy of Arts
1 Shipka Street
Alexander Smirnov
1907

073
CE

The State School for Painting was inaugurated in Sofia back in 1896. The project for a new school was commissioned to the Russian architect Alexander Smirnov in 1905 after a competition. The project encompassed the entire urban block to the south-east of St Alexander Nevski Cathedral. The building, which today houses the National Academy of Arts, was finished in 1907. The Austrian architect Friedrich Schwamberg, who was in charge of the construction management, died during the works. The building is a Secessionist interpretation of Byzantine architecture, combined with elements of traditional Russian church architecture from the 16th century. This is expressed in the ogee arches on the second floor. The roots of this type of arch can be traced back to Rome and the Middle East and the Oriental influences on early Gothic architecture, in particular in Venice, from where it spread across Europe and became known as the 'Venetian arch'.

View towards the National Library (074) and Sofia University (081)

074

Saints Cyril and Methodius National Library

074

CE

88 Vasil Levski Boulevard
Ivan Vasilyov, Dimitar Tsolov.
Sculpture: Mihaylo Parashchuk.
Monument of Saints Cyril and Methodius: Vladimir Ginovski, Ivan Ivanchev
1957, 1972 (monument)

The establishing of the National Library in 1879 was an initiative of the teacher Mikhail Bobotinov. The plot was once the royal *manège* (horse-riding arena). The library, which today houses more than seven million books, was designed in 1935 in the spirit of interwar monumental classicism. Construction started in 1939, but was postponed until the end of the Second World War. Therefore, the work of the architects became symbolic of the contradictory political circumstances from the 1930s to the Stalinist period. The building is located on the Sofia Ring Road and is an important part of the ensemble of representative buildings in the area, such as the University of Sofia, the National Academy of Arts, the National Assembly, St Alexander Nevski Memorial Cathedral, and others. Its meaning is intensified by the large green

open spaces that surround it and are connected to the Doctors' Garden (see 078). The library's appearance is monumental and ceremonious. A colonnade forms the main elevation and the entrance. The interior is dominated by marble columns, marble wall-cladding, *muschelkalk* limestone, and wooden panelling. In the centre of the front garden, as though leading to the entrance, is the bronze monument in honour of the saint brothers from Thessaloniki who created the Slavic alphabet, Cyril and Methodius. Saint Cyril died on 14 February 869 and was buried in the Basilica of Saint Clemente in Rome. His younger brother Saint Methodius died on 6 April 885 and was buried in the central church of Velehrad, which is today in the Czech Republic. In 1980 Pope John Paul II declared the two saints co-patrons of Europe.

Residence of the Ambassador of the Republic of Turkey
119 Tsar Osvoboditel Boulevard
Friedrich Grünanger
1903

075
CE

This building has preserved the authentic shape and the historic atmosphere connected with the stay of Mustafa Kemal Atatürk, the founder of the Republic of Turkey, as the military attaché in Sofia. It was initially erected as the private house of a prominent Bulgarian politician and diplomat. The eclectic mixture of the façades is based on a neo-baroque composition. The splendid interior decor and furniture are remarkable – in particular the entrance foyer with its glass paintings, chimney, and gilded cupboard. The reception halls were furnished in the style of Louis XV of France. All of the furniture, the gilded crystal chandeliers, and the Baccarat vases were brought from Istanbul in the 1930s. The interior is completed with the parquet, ornamented with various kinds of wood, and by the skilfully chosen Turkish carpets and fine artworks. Of a special interest is the cabinet used by Fethi Okyar – a military attaché and ambassador who later became prime minister of the Republic of Turkey – with its monumental oak desk, encrusted table, and rich library.

Maxim private club (former Yablanski residence)

076

CE

18 Tsar Osvoboditel Boulevard
Friedrich Grünanger. Restoration: Georgi Ugrinov, Ilka Dishlieva
1907, 2010 (restoration)

The house was initially built as a private residence for Dimitar Yablanski, a wealthy businessman and the mayor of Sofia from 1897 to 1899. It is an example of the neo-baroque influences after the Liberation in 1878 and one of the highest achievements of architecture in the 1900s. The style is clearly related to that of the Royal Palace, as the same architect designed both structures. The silhouette is defined by the mansard roof and the attics of the protruding central elements, while a sculptural cornice runs along the entire building. The entrance portico is oriented to the court on the western side, but the most impressive elevation is the eastern one with the garden-terrace. Some Rococo-style stucco ornaments embellish the interiors. The building was used as an embassy after the Second World War. From 1989 it changed owners numerous times and fell into ruin, until it was finally restored and converted into a private club.

Apartment building with banks and offices ↓

077

CE

1 Stara Planina Street/
111 Georgi Sava Rakovski Street
Alexander Dubovik
1939

The building is located on a corner directly opposite the National Opera. Its simple and compact volume is interrupted by an additional storey at the corner. A simple canopy completes its horizontal articulation. The exterior design leaves the office function in the mezzanine almost

unexpressed. The building is one of the very rare examples of extreme functionalism. The only structuring elements are the alternating horizontal strips of windows and the wall surfaces, promoting a straightforward model from the modernist cannon. The architecture of the edifice represents, through its author, the impact of Czech interwar functionalism, which helped transmit the influence of the Bauhaus to architecture in Bulgaria.

Doctors' Monument and Gardens ↑

078
CE

Shipka Street, Oborishte Street
Doctors' Monument:
Antonin Tomisek/Tomichko, Luigi Farabosko; 1884
Doctors' Garden:
Daniel and Karl Neff, Hristo Mihov; 1889.
Georgi Duhtev; 1936
Garden of the Prince's Circus:
Baron Ebner von Eschenbach, Emil Amann; 1896

The monument is dedicated to the doctors and other medical staff who lost their lives in the Russian-Turkish Liberation War in 1877–1878. Its shape has its origin in the ancient symbol of the pyramid. The large stone blocks with inscribed names, and the Byzantine columns of the sarcophagus, which crowns the monument, situate it in the Romantic wave of monumental arts at that time. Its chosen location respected the pre-existing green area of Prince's Circus to the west. The monument became a defining element of the gardens.

Prince Alexander I Battenberg Tomb-Monument ↓

079
CE

81 Vasil Levski Boulevard
Jakob Heinrich Meyer
1897

Alexander von Battenberg (1857–1893) was the Prince of Bulgaria after liberation from Ottoman rule. The most important political event during his reign was the unification of the Bulgaria Principality with the autonomous region of Eastern Rumelia in 1885. The prince had to abdicate after a military putsch on 26 August 1886 and moved to Graz, Austria, as Graf von Hartenau. Upon his death the Bulgarian government took the decision to build a tomb for his mortal remains. The design was assigned to the Swiss architect Jakob Heinrich Meyer, who used a version of a neo-baroque design language. Above the main entrance is the prince's personal coat of arms, which at that time was also the State's. The decoration, which initially consisted of art nouveau motifs, is by the Bulgarian artist Haralampy Tatchev.

St Paraskeva Church
58 Georgi Sava Rakovski Street
Anton Tornyov. Iconostasis: Todor Hristov, Ivan Travnicki
1930, 1940 (iconostasis)

080
CE

The edifice is a unique example of religious architecture in Bulgaria – in terms of its tectonic and spatial structure, as well as in its national interpretation of the Byzantine architectural tradition. The design invented a new model of organic symbiosis between tradition and innovation: a religious space, formed by a modernist aesthetic concept and realised with the most innovative technologies of the time, but building upon a centuries-old archetype for architectural and plastic details. The church is a single-space building, based on the combination of a square

and an octagon and covered by a dome with a diameter of 20 metres. There is a gradual transition from bottom to top in several rings visible in the exterior: from a square to an octagon, then to a hexadecagon (16-sided polygon), and finally to the circular drum of the dome. The inner transition between the polygons is achieved through corner arches similar to squinches. The single-space solution was driven by the need for a direct visual link to the ritual; the view would otherwise be hindered by the columns. The entire structure was cast in concrete, and the main dome is a concrete shell. The walls are covered with cement bricks, and the cornices are of artificial stone, all cast in place. The elevations are densely and discretely decorated with animistic and fantastic imagery, expressed in stone carving and iron meshwork expressing a fairy tale. One noteworthy element is the curvilinear cornice above the dome, which is reminiscent of those in Bulgarian houses of the 19th century. In his endeavours to discover a new national form in architecture, Anton Tornyov reconsidered many of the postulates in Orthodox architecture, recreating a tradition that had been oppressed for nearly five centuries.

View towards St Paraskeva Church

Sofia University and Library

081

CE

15 Tsar Osvoboditel Boulevard
Henri Bréançon, Nikola Lazarov. Eastern and northern wings: Lyuben Konstantinov. Spas Rangelov. Library: Ivan Vasilyov, Dimitar Tsolov. Lion figures: Lyuben Dimitrov
1906, 1934 (lion figures),
1952 (eastern and northern wings), 1985

The construction of the complex of Sofia University 'St Kliment Ohridski' complex lasted over a long period: from 1906 to 1985. The initial design for the Rectorate building was the winning entry in an international competition held in 1906. The project was revised twice – in 1910 and 1924 – and finished in 1934. The architectural language changed throughout the different planning phases: it began as French neoclassical, but the final result included neo-baroque and neo-Renaissance features both on the exterior and in the interior. The building was severely damaged in the Second World War, when some of the valuable stained-glass was destroyed, and then restored in 1983. The University Library was erected in 1934 in a romanticist spirit with art-deco elements and an expressive convex wall surface at the main entrance. The delicate use of

classicist details in the rational elevation design bears the sentiment of integrity between two works created at different times and according to different artistic concepts. The inner spaces are decorated with a mixture of neo-Byzantine and neo-classical architectural details. The extension of the Rectorate with two side wings lasted from 1952 to 1985. The architecture of the wings differs from the initial design idea for a complex of pavilions, but it continued the classicist and baroque representativeness of the building. The persistent stylistic endeavours in search of an image for the building were fostered by the political context throughout the 1950s.

View towards Sofia University

081

Moskovska 37 cooperative apartment building

082

CE

37 Moskovska Street
Viktoria Angelova-Vinarova
1937

In the 1930s and 1940s a great number of multi-storey apartment buildings were erected in Sofia, especially in the centre. This is a fine example – not only of a façade but also of a floor plan. Every apartment is clearly separated into three functional areas – the living space, bedrooms, and service rooms. In each, the rooms are grouped around a central vestibule, which serves as an entrance space. The two front doors are also separated – one is the official entrance, and the other is a service one. The façade is in the spirit of 1930s: the horizontality of the wide windows is amplified by the balconies. The small detail of the decorative consoles underneath the balconies is a clear reference to a double-curved form that is typical in Bulgarian vernacular architecture. The area in front of the recessed main entrance door is finely decorated with coloured tiles.

St Sofia cooperative apartment building

083

CE

27–29 Moskovska Street

Lazar Parashkevanov

1929

Eight storeys high and in the very heart of the city – at the top of the sacral hill and metres away from St Sofia Church – this building had to be grand. It later became an important point of reference for the large-scale shaping of the silhouette of Moskovska Street. The axis of symmetry on the southern elevation shown above is emphasised by an attic floor. The architecture is well proportioned and sculpturally structured by the windows and balconies. The curved corners and balconies continuously connect the design of the main elevation to that of the secondary ones. The iron railings of the balconies and the balustrades of Ionic columns in the corners round off the design. The building is one of the first examples of a cooperative housing development in Bulgaria. The architecture was influenced by the art nouveau style of the interwar period.

DSK Bank (former Bank of Sofia, State Savings Bank)

084

CE

19 Moskovska Street/
Georgi Benkovski Street
Georgi Fingov, Dimo Nichev, Nikola Jurukov. Sculptor: Marin Vassilev. Extension: Zdravka Shtiliyanova
1913, 2010 (extension)

The programme of the building was for bank offices and apartments for the bank directors. Set on the corner between two streets, the edifice clearly shows off its diverse influences: art nouveau mixed with elements of baroque. The elevations are embellished with curved *avant-corps*, as well as sculptural compositions: statues of eagles and seated figures above the entrance and the figure of Mercury, the Roman god of trade, at the corner. The building's simple and elegant extension from 2010, which runs along Georgi Benkovski Street, acts as a neutral backdrop, highlighting the intricate façades of the original structure.

State Insurance Company (former Clerical Cooperative Savings & Insurance Company)

085

CE

6 Tsar Osvoboditel Boulevard/
3 Georgi Benkovski Street
Georgi Fingov, Dimo Nichev, Georgi Yurukov. Sculptures on dome: Toma Deliradev. Reconstruction of north façade: Stancho Belkovski, Ivan Danchov
1926, 1937 (north façade reconstruction)

After the First World War the average building height in Sofia city centre grew from two to seven floors. This edifice shows the new height. Part of the building's original façade can be seen along Georgi Benkovski Street. Its style is neo-baroque from the end of the 19th century with Secession influences. The building's second owner asked that it be altered in accordance with the rationalist architecture of the Bulgaria Hotel next to it. Thus, the corner and the elevation along Tsar Osvoboditel Boulevard were redesigned by the authors of the hotel in the spirit of modernised classicism in 1937.

National Gallery – Square 500 (former State Printing House, former National Gallery for Foreign Arts, and former State Polytechnic building)

086

CE

1 19th February Street/
Alexander Nevski Square
State Printing House:
Friedrich Schwamberg, Jakob Heinrich Meyer; 1884, 1897
State Polytechnic buildings:
1952
National Gallery for Foreign Arts:
Nikola Nikolov, Liliana Stoynova; 1987
Reconstruction, new courtyard:
Yanko Apostolov, Tsvyatko Penev, Mira Halan, Nikolay Borisov; 2015

The new National Gallery is a group of several buildings, parts, and segments, which were all constructed at different times and then finally united into one complex after a series of competitions initiated by the Ministry of Culture from 2013 to 2015. The intention was to bring together under one roof several art collections of national significance. The State Printing House on the western side was built in the spirit of Viennese neobaroque, but destroyed by air raids during the Second World War. In 1987, around 100 years after its erection, it was rebuilt as a museum. Lyudmila Zhivkova, daughter of the totalitarian leader and the Minister of Culture at the time, insisted on establishing the National Gallery for Foreign Art to house the new State's collection of art from around the world. Nikola Nikolov's design replaced the mansard roof with a completely closed sky-lit third floor. On the outside sculptural figures, vases, and other ornaments decorated the building. The height of the two corner volumes was raised to correspond to that of the central volume. The concave curves of the old roof were replaced by convex ones and the dormers were retained. The historic interpretation is

a late-Romantic citation, which should be regarded in the postmodern context of the time. After an international competition for their reconstruction and adaptation, the various parts of the complex and the inner courtyard between them were synthesised into one design solution. This was won by the US-based architect of Bulgarian origin Yanko Apostolov. As part of the general concept for a new National Gallery, the State Polytechnic on the eastern side was reconstructed in 2015 with respect to the authentic elevations and limited interventions in the adaptation of the interiors. The buildings define an inner court, which is integrated into the exhibition spaces. The rationalist treatment of the interior space and the central one of the court is in tune with contemporaneity as well as with its neo-historical surroundings. The court elevations create a delicate link to the authentic shape of the preserved parts and stand in dialogue with the historicism of the western side of the building, while giving the space a suitable public scale.

Embassy of the Holy See (former private house)

087

CE

6 11th August Street
Reconstruction: Todor Bulev
1895, 1966,
1994 (reconstruction)

The house was originally the property of Monsignor Angelo Giuseppe Roncalli, who was the Representative of the Holy See and Apostolic Delegate in Bulgaria from 1925 to 1934 and the future Pope John XXIII. The embassy complex consists of two buildings and a courtyard. The complex was renewed under Mario Rizzi, the Apostolic Nuncio in Bulgaria from 1991 to 1996. In the course of the renovations, a number of architectural changes were made to the interior of the main building and the elevations of the auxiliary one. The courtyard was redesigned as an interior space. As a result of these interventions, the small corner building received, next to its spiritual significance, a meaning in respect the urban structure. During his visit to Bulgaria in 2002, Pope John Paul II resided in the embassy.

Vasil Levski Monument 088 CE

Vasil Levski Square

Architect/sculptor: Adolf Václav Kolář. Relief: Rudolf R. von Weyr. Metal elements: Rudolph Philipp Waagner. Restoration: Lilia Penkova

1897, 1983 (restoration)

The monument was erected on the spot where Vasil Levski, the ideologist of the Bulgarian national uprising for liberation from Ottoman rule, was hanged. It takes the form of an obelisk set on a pedestal and has a height of 13 metres. Identical panels with architecture motifs and medallions make up the three sides of the pedestal, combining neoclassical with neo-baroque details. A portrait relief of Levski adorns the obelisk.

Sofia University Botanical Garden 089 CE

49 Moskovska Street

Daniel Neff.

Stefan Georgiev, Karl Neff

1889, 1892

The erection of the complex started immediately after Liberation. The first wing of the former First Male High School was built on the western edge of the plot, and some years later the northern wing of the school was constructed. This formed a respectable neoclassical architectural framework for the future botanical garden. The planting of this garden – the first in the country – started from the south-eastern part of the plot, on an area of 0.5 hectares, including 500 square metres of greenhouses. Over 1,500 types of rare plants can be seen in the garden, as can highlights such as two over-100-year-old oak trees, a dawn redwood imported from the Chinese province of Sichuan, and more than 40 types of roses. The garden is a member of Botanic Gardens Conservation International, the European Botanic Gardens Consortium, and the Environmental and Botanic Garden Education Network, and takes part in the Index Seminum, a worldwide seed-exchange programme. At present the garden space is used, with its basic programme, for various celebrations and official and private events – all held in its picturesque landscape.

Monument to the Soviet Army: in 2011, the sculptural relief at the base of the obelisk was used for an art installation that transformed the Soviet soldiers into comic-book characters.

Prince's Garden with Monument to the Soviet Army

090

CE

Vasil Levski Boulevard/
Tsar Osvoboditel Boulevard/
E. & H. Georgievi Boulevard/
Gen. Joseph Gurko Street
Prince's Garden:
Carl Betz. Lucien Shevalas, Johann Keller. Friedrich Grünanger. Georgi Fingov. Luben Neykov, Totyu Goranov
1882, 1887, 1893, 1903, 1936
Monument to the Soviet Army:
Danko Mitov, Ivan Vasilyov, Lyuben Neikov, Boris Kapitanov. Sculptures: Ivan Funev, Lubomir Dalchev, Mara Georgieva, Vaska Emanouilova, Vassil Zidarov, Petar Doychinov

The creation of the garden was initiated by Prince Alexander I Battenberg. The first step was the formation of a neoclassical composition in the south-western part of the area at the end of the 19th century. The garden's design changed radically at the beginning of the 20th century, when the prince's zoological garden was located in the southern part and a botanical garden was added to the north. The old section of the garden with the zoo was destroyed during the Second World War. The zoo was later restored and existed there until the 1980s, when it was moved to another part of the city. The Monument to the Soviet Army was erected at the centre of the garden, fixed by the basic compositional axes. It was an expression of the new political context, but its design was an interpretation of a historically established composition of architectural elements, such as massive proportions, a low ziggurat with reliefs, and an obelisk crowned by a sculptural composition. The sculptural relief at the base of the obelisk, which presents Soviet soldiers supported by local antifascist partisan troops, has been used for various art installations (see pages 154–155).

Angel Kantardzhiev's house
Behind 25 Tsar Osvoboditel Boulevard
Ivan Vasilyov, Dimitar Tsolov
1932

091
CE

Among the most impressive instances of the residences of wealthy families in Sofia is Angel Kantardzhiev's house, designed by Ivan Vasilyov and Dimitar Tsolov. The architectural duo were well-known for their interwar projects – important public buildings with a particular combination of local traditions and neoclassical features. Examples include the National Bank, the National Library, and St Nedelya Church. In the design for this house, they demonstrated their detailed knowledge of the architectural language of the Modern Movement, implementing a flat roof, terraces, simple geometric volumes, and wide windows. The house is one of the few examples of a free-standing building in the urbanised centre of Sofia. The design of its interior follows a holistic approach with a full set of built-in furniture designed and produced particularly for the building. Constructivist and neo-plasticist features show the architects' free interpretations of the trends of the time.

Sense Hotel

092

CE

16 Tsar Osvoboditel Boulevard
Lazzarini Pickering Architetti, Tzonkov Architectural Group
2013

Surrounded by historic buildings, the silhouette of the Sense Hotel has a strong presence on Sofia's most distinctive boulevard, the yellow-paved Tsar Osvoboditel. The architectural project for the hotel implemented a dynamic façade that reflects the vitality of the area. The non-uniform grid of the street-facing façade becomes three dimensional for the three upper levels, thus creating pergolas above the recessed terraces. The shiny glass structure sets a counterpoint to its historical surroundings. Pivoting brass panels make up the inner layer of the façade, providing a constantly changing shiny surface and at the same time acting as a screen for the bedrooms. The subdued palette of materials in the interior, which includes wooden floors and leather upholstery, creates a minimalist, rather masculine look. When opened, the brass shutters in each of the 71 bedrooms reveal floor-to-ceiling glass windows and views towards the Parliament and the golden domes of St Alexander Nevski Memorial Cathedral.

Central Military Club (former Sofia Military Officers' Assembly)

093

CE

7 Tsar Osvoboditel Boulevard
Adolf Václav Kolář.
Nikola Lazarov, Friedrich Grünanger.
Decoration: Marin Vassilev
1898, 1903 (decoration)

The club was the main focal point for public life in Sofia around 1900. As a mixed-use building, its complicated functional concept is characterised by a flexibility more typical of later architectural concepts. This was in opposition to the amphilade planning variations and symmetrical corridors usual for the time. The building's plan made it possible for different sections to function separately or to be joined together for large events. It could be claimed that this was Bulgarian architecture's first step towards rationalism in the planning of public buildings – a style whose possibilities were more fully explored later, in the 1920s. The open plan defines the three-dimensional composition and influences the tectonic structure. Two grades of rustication cover the neo-Renaissance elevation. The original set-back passway on the ground level, the deep loggia above, and the open terrace on the third level all link the interior spaces to an important city boulevard. The openness to the public spaces outside completes the atmosphere of the interior, which is enriched with small-scale eclectic decor with neo-Renaissance, classicist, Rococo, and neo-baroque features. The complicated functional and formal system successfully addressed both the austerity of the military institution and the euphoric expectations held at the turn of the 19th century.

Ministry Of Youth And Sports (Sports Palace) 094 CE
75 Vasil Levski Boulevard
Angel Damyanov. Sculptures: Alexandar Haytov, Zdravec Haytov
1955, 2014 (sculptures)

The edifice was part of an extensive programme of new governmental buildings in the first decade after the Second World War. Its functional programme followed some practical considerations: to attach to the administrative section to a covered swimming pool with its adjacent services. The design adhered to the formula of the socialist historicism of the time. The main, representative elevation, which faces Vasil Levski Boulevard, dominates all of the other views towards the building. Despite the overall classicist image of the so-called Sports Palace, the elongated proportions of the arches in the attic recall Italian rationalism. On the urban level the ministry is situated in such a way that it lies upon the same axis as the Vasil Levski National Stadium across Knyazheska Garden. The two buildings were intended for construction at the same time.

Slavyanska Beseda Complex 095 CE
127 Georgi Sava Rakovski Street, 3 Slavyanska Street
Assen Mihaylovski, Georgi Apostolov, Vladimir Branekov
1935

This complex with entrances on Georgi Sava Rakovski and Slavyanska streets was built by a public association named Slavyanska Beseda, which was founded in 1880. It was the first construction erected by the association, an important cultural institution which founded the first State Theatre and the Opera

troupe. The building complex has several different functions: a hotel with a cafe, the Salza i Smyah ('Tears and Laughter') Theatre, an exhibition hall, and some retail space. The design refrains from subdividing the compact volume into parts. The elevations are structured only by the straight ordering of the windows. Their simplicity is slightly interrupted by the small, vertically arranged balconies. The top floor is recessed, leaving space for a terrace with thin metal railings and a canopy, which casts a deep shadow and completes the façade. The architectural language is one of calm rationalism.

Apartment building

096

CE

6 6th September Street/
5 Slavyanska Street
Georgi Ovcharov
1929

The building was one of the first cooperative housing developments. As its architect, who was already well-known at the time, owned an apartment and lived there with his family, it is also known as Georgi Ovcharov's Cooperative. The viewer's first impression of the architecture comes from its large proportions. The high oriel bay windows are paired with arches beneath a cornice, thus organising the oriel motifs in big, rhythmic steps and intensifying the monumentality. The façade materials are plaster and brick, with the latter used extensively on the ground floor and as framing for the windows and arches on the upper levels. The ground floor is further elaborated with structural and decorative details. Above the entrances, in the axes of the arches, are protruding sculptures of lions' heads made by the architect. Despite the different typologies and sizes of this building and that of the Faculty of Agronomy, created by the same architect, the similarity between the two edifices is clearly recognisable.

Centre to West

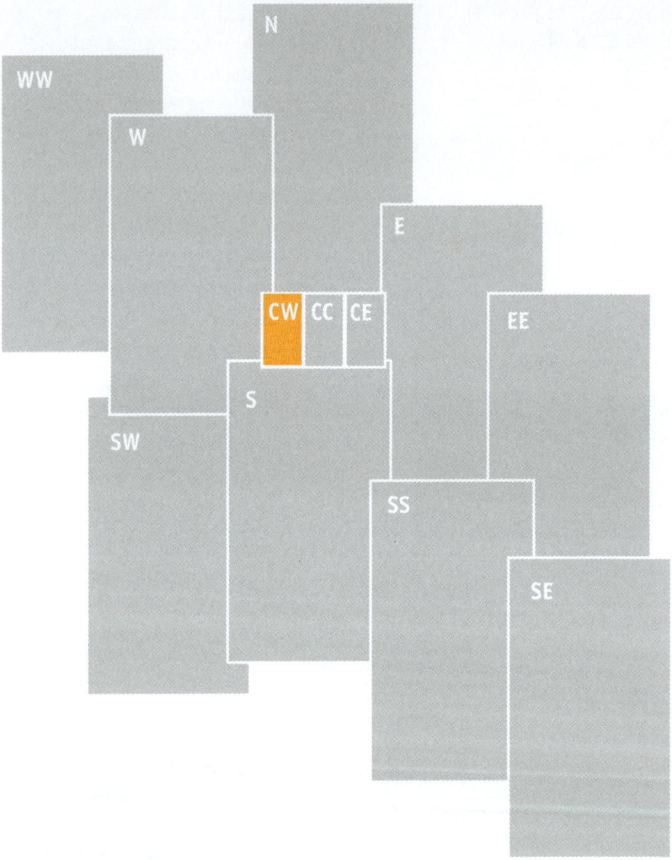

Map CW

The area encloses the western parts of the Ottoman inner city and the undeveloped areas between the Roman fortification trench and the Vladayska River. It was radically structured by an orthogonal street grid, popular at the end of the 19th century as the American regulation. It was the first step towards the extensive urban development of the capital city. The social and cultural context of the area was defined by the multiethnic population of Bulgarians, Jews, Armenians, and Roma. A great number of refugees from Macedonia, Thracia, and Dobrudja settled in the area as a result of the wars at the beginning of the 20th century, as did Russian emigrants after the Russian Revolution. The rapid population increase in the city to 140,000 inhabitants in 1920 was the main reason for the development of the area. The multicoloured social and cultural structure consisted of retailers, traders, and workers of a lower social status. The reconstruction of the area started in the 1980s and marked the beginning of the extension of the city centre westwards. The final step in the orientation of the centre to the west was the realisation of Todor Alexandrov Boulevard in the 1990s.

Hotel Rodina

097

CW

8 Gen. E. I. Totleben Boulevard
Todor Kojuharov, Evlogui Tsvetkov, Luben Traykov, Anton Hadjidinev. Civil Engineer: Preslav Hadjov
1984

Hotel Rodina is situated on one of Sofia's main radial boulevards. The building stands on the back part of the plot, away from the boulevard, thus offering space for a piazza and a car park in front. At 105 metres tall, it was the highest building in the city at the time of construction. The hotel offered rooms and apartments, and included 1,050 beds in total, a restaurant with 450 seats, and large foyers with shops and a cafeteria, as well as conference halls and a swimming pool. The main foyer is organised around an atrium space which connects the first two floors in a single public space. The grid on the dark-coloured façades is derived from the prefabricated modular panels of the cladding.

Russian Monument

098

CW

Ruski Pametnik Square
Vladimir Sherwood. Construction: Vokar
1882

This monument was the first one erected in Sofia in honour of the Russian emperor Alexander II and Bulgaria's liberation from the Ottoman Empire. It is located on the road by which the Ottoman officer Osman Nuri Pasha fled the city when the Russian army arrived on 22 December 1877. On the western side of the pedestal are the dates of the Russian-Turkish War (1877–1878), and a shortened passage from the Bible, which reads 'not to us, not to us, but to Your name...'. This citation was inscribed on Russian medals during the Napoleonic Wars in 1812 and the Russian-Turkish War. The 10-metre-high monument takes the form of an obelisk upon a high pedestal. The obelisk shape originates from Ancient Egypt (2500 BCE) and symbolises the rays of the sun. It was widely used during the 18th and 19th centuries in Europe and America and was established as a sign of respect for historic events and persons.

Ministry of Agriculture, Food and Forestry

099

CW

55 Hristo Botev Boulevard
Nikola Lazarov, Ilia Popov
1927

The plot has a slight northward slope, and so the main entrance is located on the curved corner facing Macedonia Square, which is a focal point in Sofia. The corner is flanked by two pseudo-baroque towers crowned with pointed roofs and classicist fragments. Its grandeur is further emphasised by the sculptural details of the balconies and the large window openings on the first floor. The main fronts along the boulevard and the street are embellished with decorative chains of fruits and flowers, medallions, cornices, and intricate window frames. The interiors are shaped with plaster ceilings, rosettes, decorative panels, a marble staircase with an iron banister, and colourful mosaics. The monumental appearance of the curved entrance section and the compositional effect of the tower accents suffered after a later addition of a roof floor. As a result, the central curved part seems much lower today than the rest of the building. The project for the Ministry of Agriculture, Food and Forestry was devised before the First World War and so is a typical example of the European eclectic historicism of the late-19th-century post-liberation period in Bulgaria.

Urban Module

100

CW

Aleksandar Stamboliyski Boulevard/Shar Planina Street
AEDES Studio/Plamen Bratkov, Rossitsa Bratkova
2013

The Urban Module (UM) office building is situated on Aleksandar Stamboliyski Boulevard, which begins at St Nedelya Church at the very centre of Sofia. After the National Insurance Institute, the 15-storey tower is the second high-rise along that urban axis. Based on its composition and its white local stone, which stand in contrast to the horizontality of the shopping mall on the opposite side of the boulevard and respect the details of the next-door Stalinist school building, UM is firmly connected to the local context. The design commenced with a simple combination of slabs and columns. Broken down through the prism of Modernity, they became signs of prefabrication, resembling double T-panels. To interact with the details of the neighbouring school building, joints were placed at the middle of each element, dividing the volume into smaller parts. The new structure was then exposed to forces of attraction and repulsion – each in its own direction – adding some individuality to the repeating offices. Thus, the slabs and columns shifted in different ways, yet remained parts of the whole. The alternating volumes evoke the idea of an ongoing process: the windows shift back and forth, and the regularity of the façade is randomly interrupted by solid niches instead of glazing between elements. The depth of the columns allowed the architects to improve the solar shading, which adds to the sustainability of the building. On both sides of the tower, intermediate elements provide a smooth connection to the existing residential buildings.

Mall of Sofia →

101

CW

101 Aleksandar Stamboliyski Boulevard
Plamen Nanov, Milena Nanova, Yordan Likov, Plamen Mihaylov, MYS Architects
2006

Located in the city centre, the Mall of Sofia was the first modern mixed-use shopping centre in Bulgaria. It has three retail floors, a five-storey office building with a separate entrance, and three underground parking levels. The mall is divided into two sections – a straight and a curved one – in order to make full use of the available space and to provide continuity in walking routes through the building, good visibility for shopfronts, and easy orientation for visitors. There is an equal distribution of commercial areas and additional space for the anchor shops located on the corners. There is a film complex, a food court,

and a restaurant on the top floor of the shopping centre. Cinema City consists of 12 screens and the first IMAX cinema in the country. The full-height glazed façades provide views of the surrounding area, as do the seating areas of the food court and the restaurant. The retail area extends below ground level, with a supermarket and other shops organised around a small secondary mall. The building stands at the crossroads of two main boulevards (Aleksandar Stamboliyski and General Mihail D. Skobelev), and its shape corresponds to the scale of the surrounding urban blocks. Clearly defined volumes shape the corners of the building and direct attention towards the main entrances to the mall. The office tower on top of the shopping centre, which has long, horizontal proportions, took its lines from the existing silhouette of the street.

St George the Victorious Church 102 CW

90 Patriarch Evtimiy Boulevard
Anton Tornyov. Icons in interior: Gospodin Zhelyazkov. Iconostasis: Balachev. Carved wooden thrones: Philip Filipov
1918, 1930 (icons in interior), 1941 (carved thrones)

The church stands at the centre of a small garden. Its plan is based on the traditional principles of the cross-dome typology. The narthex is symmetrically flanked by two bell towers. Both the main and the southern entrances are covered by small canopies carried by Byzantine columns. The decoration on the elevations is reduced to some small arched-windows and a frieze of stylised floral elements below the cornice, underneath which is a strip of decorative arches. The combination of the modest Byzantine style with some Romanesque elements strengthens the Romantic vision of the architecture. The building is an early example of National Romantic style in Bulgarian architecture, and a modernised interpretation of Orthodox church architecture. The same formal language was further explored in the National Romantic architecture of the 1930s.

St Nikolay Sofijski Church
76 Pirotska Street/
Opalchenska Street
Anton Tornyov.
Iconostasis: N. and L. Alexievi
1900

103
CW

Named after Nikolay Martinov, a 16th-century Christian martyr, this church is the second largest in Sofia. Its construction was initiated by the city's citizens and was realised with donations, including a considerable one from the Russian tsar. The plan is based on the traditional cross-dome typology. The two symmetrical bell-towers flanking the narthex are not common in Orthodox churches. The covered entrances are accentuated by the Byzantine-style columns. As a reference to the churches from the Second Bulgarian Empire, the elevations are lined with horizontal ceramic strips, and there is a frieze depicting birds and grapevines. The interior is dominated by the wooden iconostasis, which was carved by successors of the Debar woodcarving school. The church is an instance of National Romanticism and a listed cultural monument.

Independent Trade Union of Builders (former Carpenters' Guild building)

104

CW

71 Hristo Botev Boulevard
Anton Tornyov.
Sculpture panel: Alexander Andreev.
Stonecutting: Georgi Kiselinchev
1910

The object was initially erected for the Guild of Bulgarian Carpenters in Sofia. It has since been used by different construction-workers' guilds and has therefore been known as the Bricklayers' Building. The intended purpose of the building was expressed by an imposing panel of 3 × 13 metres, depicting construction activities in Sofia. The integration of the panel into the architecture was the first significant example of a synthesis between architecture and sculpture in Bulgaria. The panel expressed labour scenes appropriate for 19–20th-century art, while its morphology links the imagery to the language of the then-contemporary Secessionist movement. The topic was treated realistically, presenting a scene of an ancient epos in the universal language of a Bible proverb. The picturesque effect of the shallow relief, the aesthetic integrity of the decorative panel, and the tectonic structure of the architecture recall Richard Wagner's concept of a *Gesamtkunstwerk* ('total art work').

First Evangelical Church ↑

105
CW

49 Solunska Street
Vatclav Krasny
1886

The Evangelical movement started in Bulgaria in the middle of the 19th century. This single-nave church, with a pointed roof tower above the entrance was influenced by the neo-Romanesque trends in Europe at the end of the 19th century. The church was destroyed in 1944 and rebuilt after the Second World War.

Jewish Cultural Centre ↓

106
CW

50 Aleksandar Stamboliyski Boulevard/Vazrajdane Square
Baruh Baruh
1930

The building is set on a corner and it has a public space in front of it. It was erected for the needs of the Organisation of the Jews in Bulgaria and also initially sheltered the Jewish-owned Geula Bank. The cubic volume of the corner is higher than the rest of the building. The entrance in the eastern façade is balanced by the balcony along the boulevard. The plastic frames of the pointed arches of the windows on the upper floors are the only decorative elements on the elevations. The two-storey openings at the centre of the southern elevation are the windows of the auditorium. Round windows conclude the symmetry of the façade. The initial proportions of the building, which followed a classical tripartite composition, were changed around 1990 by an additional storey. As a counterpoint to the relatively modest exterior, the interiors are much more grand. The building – where modernised classicist architecture meets features such as Romantic, pointed window-arches – is a typical example of the stylistic plurality around in the city of Sofia during the interwar period.

Eastern Zone

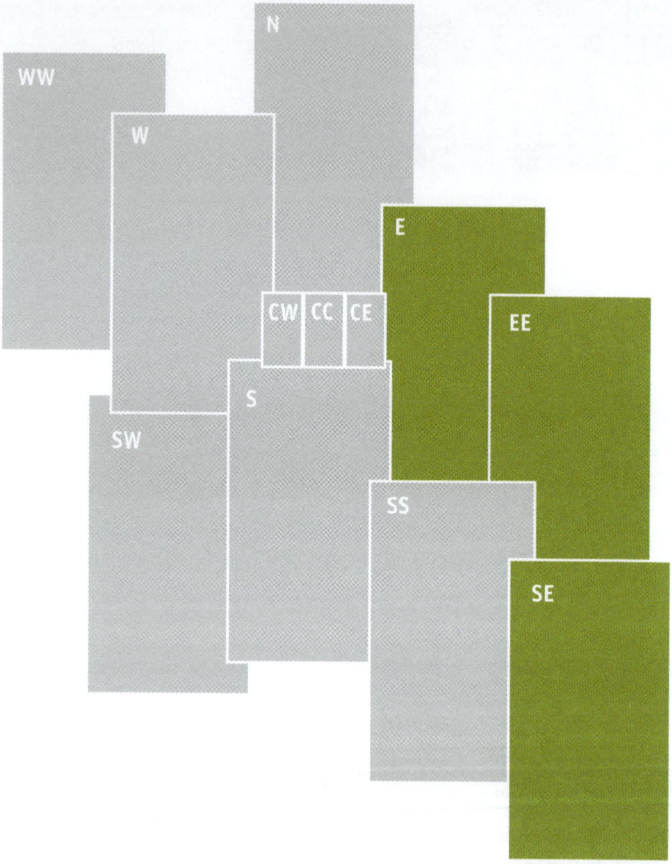

Maps SE, EE, E

The urban expansion between the radial continuations of Knyaz Dondukov Boulevard and Graf Ignatiev Street had already begun at the end of the 19th century. The in-between arterial road Tsarigradsko Chaussee became established as the main axis of development to the east. New urban quarters started developing on its north-eastern side at the beginning of the 20th century. Simultaneously, the Borisova Gradina park acquired its shape on the south-western side of the chaussee. The layout of the park was an important planning decision, which enabled the connection of the urbanised territory with the surrounding mountain slopes. That idea was developed in 1938 when Alfred Mussmann created his urban plan for the city. The plan also defined the territories of the other main green elements of the city, such as the South and West parks, the extension of the Central Cemetery to the north, and the linking of the four green areas with a green belt along the ring railway line. The plan was an interpretation of the concept of a garden city and was to be implemented after the Second World War. The eastern area was developed as complex housing after the 1950s. Over recent decades, extensive mixed-use developments have sprung up along both sides of Tsarigradsko Chaussee. The overall architectural image of the area consists of different examples of socialist modernism, some instances from the Stalinist era, and various buildings from the contemporary post-socialist period.

107

The Mound of Brotherhood Monument (see 107), erected in 1956, is dedicated to those who died in the Bulgarian uprising in 1923 and Red Army offensives in the Second World War. It establishes a strong central axis in the Borisova Gradina park.

Boris's Garden (Borisova Gradina)

107

E

1 Tsarigradsko Chaussee
Daniel Neff, Karl Neff, Emil Aman. Josef Frey. Georgi Nikolov. Georgi Duhtev. Reconstruction: Delcho Sugarev, Ivan Ivanchev, R. Ivanov, Milko Bichev. Georgi Radoslavov
1884, 1906, 1933, 1934, 1950 and 1986 (reconstruction)

The layout of the park was started in 1884 with a garden design for an area of 30 hectares, south of Eagles' Bridge. The name Borisova Gradina ('Boris's Garden') was given in 1895, on the occasion of the first birthday of the young Prince Boris. The park's basic composition was a combination of a rectangular grid of alleys and the picturesque English style of landscaping, with its organic network of pathways and artificial lakes and ponds to reflect the Romantic focus on 'natural' elements. The main entrance from Eagles' Bridge received its final shape at the end of the 19th century, when Ariana Lake was reconstructed and the garden was extended by 20 hectares. The new section was composed as a large-scale gesture in the spirit of neoclassicism. In the same period a system of sports facilities started to be developed. On the eve of the Second World War the park covered an area of about 90 hectares. The urban development plan for Sofia created by Alfred Mussmann in 1938 outlined the southern

extension of the park with a forest area which spread to the ring railway line that existed at that time. The idea was realised in 1947. That same year, the decision was taken to erect the Mound of Brotherhood Monument, a memorial to the individuals who fell in the struggle against fascism, in the area of the historic park. This changed the inherited composition but established a strong central axis for the park. The axis acquired importance, while a landscape system of alleys was developed in phases in a free-form landscape style. A redesign in the 1970s turned the entire composition of the historic part back to its Romantic roots. Today the park is the biggest in Sofia and occupies an area of around 3 square kilometres. It includes sports facilities, and recreational, cultural, and scientific objects, as well as a number of small architectural forms. The mixture of architectural and plastic artefacts is a showcase of the development of sculpture in Bulgaria from the end of the 19th century to the present day. Objects with particular significance are the Astronomical Observatory (1894), the Maria Luiza Swimming Pool (1939), the Vasil Levski National Stadium (1953), the Mound of Brotherhood (1956), the first TV tower (1959; see 124), and the Bulgarian Army Stadium (1967). A large number of monuments were erected to commemorate historic persons. These were created by famous sculptors, including Andrey Nikolov, Ivan Lazarov, Jeko Spiridonov, Trigor Agaronian, and Stefan Peichev.

Eagles' Bridge

108

E

Tsar Osvoboditel Boulevard/
Tsarigradsko Chaussee
Adolf Václav Kolář, Václav Prošek, Jrzhi/Georgi Prošek and Josef Prošek. Bronze sculpture and plastics: Rudolph Philipp Waagner
1891

The bridge crosses the Perlovska River and is a symbol of the Liberation. The imprisoned Bulgarians who fought for national independence and were set free from exile in the Diyarbakir Fortress, were welcomed here in March 1878. The bridge is one of the symbols of Sofia and has preserved its meaning. It was a mute witness to radical political changes and met many prestigious foreign guests. The symbolic key to the city was awarded here, along with the title of Honourable Citizen of Sofia. Right after the democratic changes in 1989, the bridge turned to a place for political demonstrations, the biggest among these attracting one million people. Because of urban growth, the bridge has been widened three times over the last 50 years. However, the original decoration has been preserved. The composition consists of classicist stone elements with neo-baroque metal ornamentation. The form of the four massive columns recalls the Doric architectural order from Classical Greece. At the top of each, cornices and spheres to hold the eagles. The four bronze birds are the symbolic guardians of the city. The railings and candelabrum evoke the atmosphere of the late Viennese baroque period. An important element of the artistic appearance of the ensemble was the yellow ceramic pavement, produced by the Austro-Hungarian firm Koszenbanya Teglagyar Tarsulat Pesten, a branch of the Wienerberger company, and set in 1907. However, the original paving was replaced during the extension in 1971, slightly changing the general appearance of the bridge.

Dimitar Blagoev Polygraphic Factory →
109
E
47 Tsarigradsko Chaussee
Atanas Popov
1955, 2010 (reconstruction)

The print-shop complex consists of the representative building which houses the editorial offices set along the boulevard, and the printing office, located at the back of the plot. The utilitarian architecture of the second building could not be seen from the public space, because of the surrounding trees. The design of the editorial building is an adaptation of a project for Moscow, which explains the scale and the neoclassical style of the building. The monumentality expresses the common understanding of the time that public buildings housing the political and financial institutions should have the appearance of 'palaces', while those intended for arts and sciences should be regarded as temples.

Bulgarian Telegraph Agency ↓
110
E
49 Tsarigradsko Chaussee
Evgeny Zidarov
1960

The building was the first structure to express the new directions in Bulgarian architecture after 1956. The political events that year – the 20th Congress of the Communist Party of the Soviet Union and the April Plenum of the Central Committee of the Bulgarian Communist Party – marked the break with the epoch of Stalinism. The discussions and publications under the conditions of the new political, economic, and cultural context lasted until 1958. They mainly concerned the spheres of art and literature but also offered a political backdrop for the restarting of modernist architecture. The building is a longitudinal four-storey volume with rhythmically arranged vertical windows, a late echo of neoclassicism. Both the bipartite separation into a ground and an upper part, and the post-constructivist canopy became clichés for a whole decade. A free-standing modernist spiral staircase is situated in the main foyer.

Residential building
10 Veliko Tarnovo Street
Georgi Stoichkov
1980

111
E

The building is located near the Doctors' Garden (see 078), in one Sofia's most prestigious locations. It opens to an inner green area to the south and faces a small street leading to the Garden to the north. This two-section, five-storey residential complex was designated for the high-ranking officials of the Bulgarian Communist Party, who were in power at that time. The well-balanced volumes are achieved through architectural detailing and the use of high-quality materials. The cladding is of limestone, a much-used material in that period. The diagonal concrete lattices contrast with the horizontal strips of the cladding, while the whiteness of the stone contrasts with the wooden window frames. Precast concrete grids stand at the edges of the street-facing balconies in order to provide isolation

Residential building ←

112

E

13 San Stefano Street/
Veliko Tarnovo Street
Nikola Antonov, Bogdan Tomalevski
1981

Despite its simple language, this building is an example of high-quality socialist residential construction. Its architecture mixes a late-modernist approach with regionalist features. The stone-clad volume has large glazed surfaces and recessed balconies with wooden ceilings, reminiscent of the carved ceilings of 19th-century Bulgarian houses. The ground floor is partially used for garages.

and privacy for the inhabitants. Some of the apartment units span two floor levels, with steps separating the living- and bedrooms of the residences from the dining rooms, kitchens, service, and storage spaces. An additional semi-underground garage building is accessible through an open ramp in the inner court. The large pine trees in the court contribute to the privacy of the apartments and the well-being of their inhabitants.

Serbian Embassy ↓

113

E

7 Veliko Tarnovo Street
Branco Petricic.
Structural engineer: V. Ganslop
1947

The edifice was designed in 1939; its construction finished in 1947. It is a unique example of radically simplified classicism meeting modern tradition, and to an extent fits into the postwar neo-historical architecture of the Stalinist period of socialism. The façade's proportions, articulation, and careful detailing resemble the early architecture of Giuseppe Terragni. An inner atrium forms the core of the social life of the institution.

National Health Institute (now National Centre of Infectious and Parasitic Diseases) ↑↓

114

E

26 Yanko Sakazov Boulevard

Todor Zlatev, Dimitar Koev

1932

The edifice was constructed in 1932 for a National Health Institute, funded by the Rockefeller Foundation. Its architectural language is a hybrid: modernist rationality with a classicist syntax. The entrance portico seems as though it was repeated twice in two different scales and materials. These two portico versions overlap and give a general impression of monumentality. The façade has a severe and rationalist character, which is enhanced by the extensive limestone cladding. The strict symmetry, the austere verticality of the portico entrance, and the two protruding side-volumes all create a sense of coldness and distance. To the right of the entrance is a 1938 sculpture by Ivan Funev, depicting a breastfeeding mother surrounded by infants. In the interior the three wide entrance doors lead to a large hall with columns and arches. The parapets of the stairs are decorated with brass elements. These and other sophisticated details in the inner spaces of the building reveal the influence of art-deco aesthetics.

Russian Cultural and Information Centre ↘

115

E

34 Shipka Street

Georgi Berberov, Ivo Tsolov

1975

The building is located in a central part of Sofia, with important institutions such as Sofia University and the studios of Bulgarian National Television in proximity. The fully glazed foyer unifying the different storeys marks the main entrance. The top floor, which houses service rooms, is a closed volume cantilevered above the entire building. The corridors and foyers

of the other two floors are oriented to the space of the central foyer. The wide stairs, terraces, and area between the building and the street all create a continuous link between the interior and exterior spaces. The cultural centre accommodates a large amphitheatre hall and a smaller one with a flat floor, various other halls, a library, a restaurant, a cafeteria, workshops, and offices, as well as an underground car park. On a half level between the basement and the ground floor there is a covered, naturally-lit inner court, accessible from the main foyer via a ramp and directly from the street via a separate entrance.

The building was one of the first to be finished in raw concrete after the Second World War, and was influenced by the brutalist architecture of the 1960s and 1970s. Unfortunately, much of that original brutalist appearance was destroyed in 2011 by the external insulation and repainting of the building.

Angel Kuyumdzhiyski's House (now the Residence of the Ambassador of the USA) ←

116

E

18 Veliko Tarnovo Street
Stancho Belkovski, Ivan Danchov
1936

The banker Angel Kuyumdzhiyski built his second house on the corner of Veliko Tarnovo and Vasil Aprilov streets after having commissioned the design to the architectural duo Belkovski-Danchov in the mid-1930s. The architects placed the house at the edge of the plot and at the meeting point of the two streets in order to leave enough space for the garden. The style of the façades also entails a meeting point – that of rational modernity and a regional version of art deco. It follows the functionality of the plan, and therefore all of the wide windows are situated on its southern façade, facing the garden. The staircases, corridors, bathrooms, and kitchen are situated to the north, and so, seen from the street, the house looks closed and solid with its few scattered windows varying in size.

Sofia Theatre

117

E

23a Yanko Sakazov Boulevard
Zheko Zhekov.
Elevation plastics: Mito Ganovski
1970

Before the current Sofia Theatre was constructed, a small theatre had been active in a multifunctional building on the opposite corner since the 1930s. The need for a larger and better-equipped auditorium led to the decision for a new building and the choice of the plot in the compositional axis of Oborishte Park (Delcho Sugarev, 1950s). The current theatre consists of a large auditorium with 300 seats and a small one with 70 seats, a well-equipped stage, and auxiliary rooms. The foyers and a cafe form a semi-closed inner court. The theatre is one of the significant examples of the late-1970s attempts to enrich the rationalist aesthetic with a more expressive plasticity. Its configuration is asymmetric and closed. The park surroundings allowed for the free modelling of the complex and well-balanced volume. The large openings to the court contrast with the massive, closed exterior. Reliefs cover the elevations. The sculptural essence of the building is further embellished by the stylobate on which it is placed. All the exterior surfaces are entirely clad in white limestone, which adds to the general appearance of a rock in its natural surroundings. The unorthodox appearance of the building was positively accepted by the theatre staff and the inhabitants of the neighbourhood.

Georgi Rakovsky Military Academy (former Military School of His Majesty) →

118

E

82 Evlogi and Hristo Georgievi Boulevard

Main building: Adolf Václav Kolář. Sculptor: Mihailo Paraschuk (1892); Reconstruction: Alexander Dubovik

1879, 1942 (reconstruction)

The main edifice of the Georgi Rakovsky Military Academy was constructed for the Military School of His Majesty, a now-defunct organisation founded in 1879. The current military academy was established in 1912. The building's design was initially a Romantic interpretation of neo-Romanesque architecture. The decoration was removed in the course of the reconstruction in 1942 and the building was clad in stone in the spirit of modernised classicism. The park and its elements were designed and realised in the Romantic tradition of the English landscape garden. The shaping of these started immediately after the erection of the main building on an area of 3 hectares, and the final composition was completed at the beginning of the 20th century. The fence surrounding the entire complex was made from the barrels of 1,895 guns, which were used during the Unification of Bulgaria in 1885.

Parushev's houses ↓

119

E

159 and 161 Evlogi and Hristo Georgievi Boulevard/ Oborishte Street

Nikola Lazarov

1911

These two houses, placed directly opposite each other, have symmetrical fronts towards the boulevard. *Avant-corps* with steep roofs are placed on the corners and on the central axes of symmetry. The two identical buildings accentuate the crossing and act as a portico along the riverbank. They are inseparable from the silhouette of the boulevard. In spite of the art-nouveau treatment of the façades, the image of the buildings gives rise to Romantic reminiscences of medieval Gothic architecture. The houses are an important example of the eclectic mix in the historicism of the late 19th century.

Expo 2000, Phase 3 and Raiffeisenbank headquarters

120

E

55 Nikola Vaptsarov Boulevard
ProArch/Maya Yovcheva
2016

Because of its strategic location, this complex – a commercial facility for rent – is easily accessible by car and public transport. Phase 3 of Expo 2000 consists of a high-rise eight-storey part and a lower three-storey section. The contemporary architecture and the dynamic silhouette contribute to the attractive and prestigious appearance of the building. The most distinctive architectural element is the façade, which combines three different treatments: a solid façade with window openings, a glazed façade, and a green façade. Sections of the roof are green areas and the vegetation continues on the eastern elevation of the lower part of the building, presenting a visual connection with the adjacent landscape. In the interior, the main entrance to the offices is designed as a two-storey-height lobby.

design presents a radical restraint from any historicist decoration. The 'sterility' of the hospital architecture and the rational aesthetic of the spaces create an ambience for almost existential meditation. In the service building of the hospital one may recognise the early style of Georgi Ovcharov, based on the references to Brick Expressionism. A polyclinic was attached to the hospital in the 1960s, connected by a closed walkway.

Queen Giovanna Hospital – Institute for Specialisation and Advanced Training of Physicians (former Queen Giovanna Workers' Hospital)

121

E

8 Byalo More Street

Georgi Ovcharov, Genko Popov

1927

The decision to build a hospital for insured workers was taken in 1927 under the patronage of Queen Giovanna of Bulgaria (1907–2000). The architecture is a late expression of European rationalism, visibly influenced by the German modernism of the 1920s. The composition of rectangular volumes follows a simple functional and structural system. The

National Tennis Centre (former Sofia Tennis Hall)

122

E

1113 Borisova Gradina

Stefka Georgieva. Structural engineers: Alfred Levie, Levcho Manuilov

1968, 2016 (reconstruction)

The tennis hall is located in the city's largest park, Borisova Gradina. The building was erected, like the Festivalna athletics hall, for the Ninth World Festival of Youth and Students in 1968. It is based on a square plan and contains tennis courts with artificial floor surfaces, tribunes, and service rooms. The roof is carried by eight frames of exposed reinforced concrete, covering a span of 37 metres and securing a clear height of 13 metres. The roof construction defines the laconic silhouette, which seems to come out of the terrain. The frames are supported by longitudinal bearings and are set over transverse bearings at the ends of the hall. The wall openings are designed as glazing on square module cassettes of wood. The pedestal zone is clad with dry masonry of natural stone. All the details and materials link to similar solutions in the neo-brutalist language and the Japanese architecture of the 1960s. The 2016 alterations, as well as changing the visible building surface to plaster, corrupted the harmony of the original architecture.

Three residential blocks ← 123 E

16–18 Frédéric Joliot-Curie Street

Stefka Georgieva

1972

Constructed in 1972 for the diplomatic corps, these three residential blocks still dominate the landscape in the quiet Iztok district. They fall among the key examples of the local brutalist trend with their dramatic silhouette. The raw reinforced concrete structure is deliberately exaggerated to interpret wooden joints, a typical feature in Bulgarian vernacular architecture. Influenced by British brutalism, Stefka Georgieva developed her brutalist creative expression in a number of buildings, which today remain among the strongest instances of this universal architectural language from the 20th century.

TV Tower ↑ 124 E

Borisova Gradina, Dragan Tsankov Blvd/Peyo Yavorov Blvd

Luben Popdonev - Genzo

1959

The TV Tower was the first one to serve the young Bulgarian National Television station. Placed upon a hill in the forest area of the Borisova Gradina ('Boris's Garden') park, it is an important accent in Sofia's urban skyline. The verticality of the slim building with 1:6 proportions is intensified by the columns set in front of the wall and the skilful vertical order of the architectural motifs. Over 14 floors, it contains different studios, workrooms, technological, and service spaces. The tower is crowned with three terraces for the broadcasting equipment and the metal structure of the antenna.

View towards the TV Tower and Borisova Gradina with Vitosha Mountain in the background

124

Universiada Hall
2 Shipchenski Prohod Boulevard
Alexander Barov, Ivan Tatarov, Doncho Vladishki, Ivan Ivanchev
1961

125
E

Bulgaria's first big hall for sports and events was realised on the occasion of the first important international sports meeting in Sofia: the Universiada international sports competition for students. The building is set back from the street, so that a large public space is formed on the western side of the plot, in front of the main entrance and foyer. The fully glazed elevation connects the foyer with the green outdoor spaces. The multifunctional hall, with a size of 36 × 30 metres, can be adapted to different sports events through a reorganisation of the seats, the use of moveable tribunes, and the various configurations of the sports field. Its capacity ranges from 2,800 to 4,800 visitors. The hall is also used for cultural events such as concerts and exhibitions. Beside the main hall there are two smaller training ones. The shape minimises the internal volume, improves the acoustics, and defines the dynamic profile of the northern and southern elevations. The contrast between the concave surface and the transparent western elevation, the inclined columns of the tribunes, the canopy above the main entrance, and, most of all, the dynamic combination of the main volume with the secondary ones, define the individual architectural character of the building. That image is achieved through the unification of the inner content with the outer shape. The hall is an emblematic example of the reborn Bulgarian modernism of the early 1960s. Even today it retains its meaning as a centre for sports and an accomplished architectural achievement.

Ministry of Foreign Affairs

126

E

2 Alexander Jendov Street

Bogdan Tomalevski, Nikola Antonov, Lozan Lozanov

1983

This is the only government building realised after the completion of the ensemble of buildings on Largo Square in the city centre in 1956. The project was commissioned to the team of three architects after a national competition held in 1975. The chosen plot continues the linear extension of the city centre to the southeast, along Tsarigradsko Chaussee. The sizes of the building are impressive for the time: the built surface spans 7,000 square metres and provides a total floor area of 35,000 square metres. The entire closed volume is 148,000 cubic metres. The main functional blocks (the representative, the administrative, and the service) form an inner court, accessible from the east through a four-storey colonnade. The representative block contains various reception and conference halls, spaces for official events, along with a restaurant, a sports hall, a cinema, and a winter garden. With spans of 7.2 and 9.6 metres, the reinforced concrete structure offers wide spaces and makes the internal layout flexible. The building is designed as a compact volume that encloses an inner court. The three-level-high open colonnade at the entrance completes the austere design of the elevation. Two of the upper floors are cantilevered from the main volume, enhancing its horizontality. The strict character of the large volumes is further elaborated in the simplicity of the secondary elements: the canopies, pylons, and window openings. The solemn interior spaces are embellished with plastic accents, wooden ceilings, and wall paintings. There is a sculpture park and exhibition space in the entrance area of the courtyard.

Asics Arena
(former Festival Hall)
35 Manastirska Street
Ivan Tatarov, Doncho Vladishki
Artists: Rossitsa Todorova,
Galin Malakchiev
1968

127
E

The former Festival Hall was constructed for the Ninth World Festival of Youth and Students, which opened in Sofia in July 1968. It is located on Slatinski Redout, one of Sofia's hills which has been populated since Antiquity. The initial idea to develop a large university sports complex was not completed and today the Hall is predominantly used for athletic events. The rhombus configuration of the plan optimises the usable size and volume (100,000 cubic metres). The steel structural beams have span distances of 20 to 60 metres. Their supports of reinforced concrete are placed in front of the elevations and turn into the main motif of the exterior composition. The plasticity of the supports visualises the structural forces running through them. A secondary structural system on the top level is based on a span of 6 × 6 metres and is coordinated with the main structure. The reinforced-concrete panels for sun protection are expressive elements and give depth to the elevation. On the two blind façades, concrete sculptural reliefs finish the overall image of the hall, which was created in the spirit of the brutalism of the 1960s. A ramp on the south-eastern side leads up to the building. In recent decades the hall has also been used to hold cultural events.

SofStock Centre
46 Professor Tsvetan Lazarov Boulevard
Ivo Petrov Architects
2014

128
EE

The complex consists of three buildings – a warehouse, an office, and service facilities – situated in a line along Professor Tsvetan Lazarov Boulevard. The sharp angles of the volumes form a recognisable and dynamic multi-winged silhouette. Access to the storage building is from the north-east over six truck ramps. With its eight storeys above-ground and one floor below-ground, the office building is the highest volume in the complex. Besides the office programme, there is a showroom on the ground floor and an educational centre and presentation halls on the third floor. The volume of the office building, with its fully glazed north façade, is protected from excessive sunlight by profiled-steel sheets placed on consoles at 80 to 100 centimetres from the main façade. The service building has four levels and is sunken into the ground on three sides. Greenery covers the entire roof, which is accessible from the fourth floor of the office building. Profiled steel sheets also cover the glazed sections on the façade of the service building.

Walltopia headquarters with training and entertainment centre

129

EE

111 Tsarigradsko Chaussee
MARSArchitects/Neville Mars. Local architects team lead: Vasil Sharlanov
2016

Walltopia is the world's biggest producer of climbing walls. In 2013 they held an international competition for the design of their headquarters. As it is part of the developing Sofia Tech Park, the Walltopia Centre shares its spaces with other innovative companies. The core of the building is the climbing centre housed in three large atriums, which divide the building volume and clearly indicate the main entrances. The three atria have glass roofs, which allow natural light to reach the innermost parts of the building. The office areas are inserted into the building space between the climbing areas as 'islands', with each of them connected to the others by bridges across the atriums. In that way, climbing becomes the unifying concept of the entire building. The façade is fully glazed to ensure maximal natural light for the offices. The triangular fragmentation of the façade and the metal structure of the glazing is a clear visual reference to Walltopia's climbing walls. The rooftop garden is a natural extension of the surrounding park.

Astral Business Centre
Christopher Columbus Blvd/
Prodan Tarakchiev Street
Atanas Panov, Sector ARCH Studio/LP Group
2011

130
EE

This Astral Business Centre stands in a strategic location just a few hundred metres away from Sofia Airport. It has a clear silhouette and a minimalist glass façade. A small square is formed at the corner in front of the entrance, which provides enough distance for the full perception of the volume and ensures the intended impression. The façade is designed as two layers of glass, the outer one unfolding as a large-scale glass fan. Apart from its aesthetics, the double skin acts as a natural protector of the inner spaces from wind and solar overheating, while also improving the ventilation of the inner spaces. The service corridor behind the façade allows easy maintenance. The main concept of the design is to create a simple volume with precise detailing. The building consists of two parts: a two-storey retail area with a showroom and a restaurant, and an eight-storey office with a height of 36 metres. Vehicle access to the two underground levels is via an open ramp from Christopher Columbus Boulevard to the south-western part of the plot. The structure of the building is reinforced concrete. The rooftop terrace acts as a kind of 'fifth façade', as it is visible from the planes taking off from and landing at Sofia Airport.

Q Centre 131 E

Tsarigradsko Chaussee/
G. M. Dimitrov Boulevard
AEDES Studio/Plamen Bratkov, Rossitsa Bratkova
2015

This office building faces one of the busiest urban motorways in Sofia. The main idea behind the design was that the building be easy to remember, even when the observer passes it at high speed. Its silhouette entirely originates from the nature of the place, and it ended up as a sort of pictogram of the activity on the road. The building stands at the spot where Tsarigradsko Chaussee intersects G. M. Dimitrov Boulevard through a roundabout in such a way that vehicles can change their direction both horizontally and vertically. The façade visualises the various possible trajectories on the roundabout as glowing ribbons that crisscross at different heights. All the office partition walls are semi-translucent, since they are made of glass bricks. The building is positioned so as to let through sunlight from the south, and therefore has an almost weightless appearance when viewed from the boulevard. The northern glass façade has several varying degrees of transparency: translucent glass and entirely or partially frosted glass with signage. This reinforces the dynamic, 'fleshless' nature of the façade. The architects regarded the façade as a graphic; the yellow surface does not carry the feel of a specific material but takes on the role of a sign, a mark.

Europark Sofia Office Centre → 132 E

40 Tsarigradsko Chaussee
Peter Tornyov, +Architectura
2005

The solitary structure stands next to one of Sofia's most important traffic routes, the connection between Sofia city centre and the international airport. The project is situated within a rough, unstructured urban district, on the border of

the Mladost housing estate and next to the city motorway. The complex consists of a main body from which the two towers rise, connected by a single vertical core. This allowed the developers to rent or sell the main body with the towers as one unit or, alternatively, as separate individual units. The structural shell of the building permits optimal utilisation and lighting of the office spaces. The different levels of the adjacent terrain are used for additional office units towards the lower part of the plot. The entrance to the office complex leads into a double-height glazed foyer with a reception on the ground floor and a small café in the gallery above. The external skin is suspended as a curtain-wall system. The longer sides of the building look like 'hole-punched' walls covered with large ceramic tiles, the colours of which vary for each office tower. The heavier appearance of the 'hole-punched' façade of the external shell creates an engrossing counterpart to the areas of light, transparent glazing on the ends of both towers.

BLU Offices
11 Brussels Boulevard
Atelier Serafimov Architects
2016

133
EE

The complex is located in a fast developing office area along a boulevard leading to the airport, and in close proximity to the large buildings of the Porsche and Maserati centres. With a striking exterior, facilities utilising advanced technology, and a sleek interior, the building has a strong presence. Its programme combines office space for rent, a hotel, and a conference centre. The edifice's slim proportions are accentuated by its glass façades with a sophisticated ventilation system. Its two volumes crowned with inclined pergolas break the 'wall' effect of the long front along the boulevard and are distinguished by their strong visibility in both directions to and from Sofia Airport. The aim of the project was the creation of a high-end – in terms of both architectural qualities and technical facilities – mixed-use complex, focused upon the coexistence of different, mutually-complementary functional groups: car parking, a hotel, and a conference block, exhibition space, and two office units.

Capital Fort Centre

90 Tsarigradsko Chaussee

A&A Architects. Concept design in partnership with WKK

2016

134

SE

Capital Fort, constructed from 2008 to 2016, is a large-scale office and retail project is situated in one of Sofia's fastest growing business districts: along Tsarigradsko Chaussee at the Bulgarian capital's south-eastern 'gate'. The project comprises a 126-metre-tall office tower and a second low-rise office building, both placed upon a podium for retail and with underground parking facilities. The building has become one of the city's new architectural landmarks. The architects carefully considered its parameters in reference to the surrounding context and the motorway. The podium of the building acts as a smooth transition between the urban environment and the office floors, and its vast, grand lobby acts as a covered public square. It serves the communication flows and provides the background for various out-of-office activities. The design of the interior public space follows the same language of dynamic and fluid forms and shapes as that of the exterior, and has a strong relationship to product design. Unconventional materials and finishes were used, and technologies taken from the automobile and ship-building industry were applied in the design and production of the winter garden, the escalators, and the main reception desk. Currently, Capital Fort is the tallest building in Bulgaria, but it will not keep its position for long. Next to it, a new 202-metre-high tower is under construction, Sky Fort.

РЕГИСТРАЦИЯ
CHECK-IN
1-24
GATES
ABC
DOMESTIC DEPARTURES

Terminal 2 of Sofia International Airport
1 Christopher Columbus Boulevard
NACO, Nl/Mathias Julius. Local architects' team lead: Dimitar Dimitrov
2007

135
EE

Terminal 2 was planned to extend Sofia Airport's capacity to around 2.6 million passengers per year. The programme includes around 100,000 square metres of covered space, of which 56,000 are dedicated to public passenger facilities and the remainder to a multilevel car park. Both the master plan and the design for new terminal were developed by the Dutch consultancy and engineering firm NACO. The inner space is defined by the rhythm of the inclined columns supporting the metal roof structure. The central glass tower, which houses the escalators that take passengers to the upper floor with the security check and departure spaces, stages the idea of a journey. Its exterior appearance recalls a pilot's cabin between two giant wings that cover the public halls of the airport space – a vision of a super jet with convexly positioned wings. Thus, the design leaves enough space for a public plaza in front of the building where all the transportation facilities are gathered. In 2014 a new station of the city metro was added to the transportation node of the building. The airport was inaugurated in 2007 for Bulgaria's entry into the European Union.

Buildings 5–8, Business Park Sofia

136

SE

Business Park Sofia, Mladost 4
A&A Architects
2007

Building 5 is one of the newest buildings in Business Park Sofia. It is located at the centre of the complex, between the older five-storey offices Building 3, and the multistorey car park P1. It faces one of the main pedestrian routes in the business park and falls at the cross-point of the existing urban grids in the complex. That situation influenced the architecture of Building 5, which has two faces – one orthogonal and solid, orientated towards the nearby buildings; and the other curved and reflective, orientated towards the centre of the business park. The curved façade represents the idea that the pedestrian flow could be calmed as a river's flow calms when running through a meander. Pedestrians slow down as they walk along the building, and so experience new things and enliven the ground-floor area. The building has different heights on each side, corresponding to the existing buildings. The transition in heights follows the logic of the two faces: it is smooth on the curved side and straight on the orthogonal one. The solid face is covered with ceramic tiles, like other buildings in the business park. Some areas of the façade are composed of specially designed vertical twisted metal strips. The same motif is repeated in the design of the reception area. The building's constantly changing appearance and distinctive silhouette make Building 5 one of the main landmarks in Business Park Sofia. Building 8 is the largest in the complex. It is located between two existing buildings: 9 and 6, which are each three times smaller than Building 8. Consequently, the main task of the design was to visually reduce the mass of the building, and to incorporate it into the surrounding context, while at the same time preserving its usable area. The architects resolved the task by dividing the building into three blocks, each with a different Tetris-like macro pattern of extrusions clad in red ceramic. The patterns give a particular character

to each block, complemented by the randomly closed external blinds. The macro pattern is also at play with the scale, because the building can be observed from a long distance away, across the complex's central park. The connection between the blocks is set back in order to leave enough space for the entrances of the building. Its façades are covered by a reflective glass curtain wall to optically enlarge the space and to dematerialize the floors. Despite its larger size, Building 8 is organically connected to the urban and architectural fabric of Business Park Sofia, and completes its spatial composition.

Banner of Peace Monument

137

SE

Kambanite Park, Bistritsa, Pancharevo

Blagoy Atanassov, Georgi Gechev. Statics engineer: Anton Maleev. Sculpture: Krum Damyanov, Mihail Benchev

1979

The monument was erected on the occasion of the first of the four Banner of Peace international children's assemblies that were held in Sofia from 1979 to 1989. The experimental forums for artistic activities and education were initiated by the Minister of Culture and daughter of the totalitarian leader Lyudmila Zhivkova. The monument is located on a green plateau outside the city, at the foot of the mountain. The plateau offers a panoramic view over Sofia, while the forest isolates it from the urban noise. The position of the monument was meant to finalise the central boulevard of the district of Mladost with a symbolic element, but because of urbanisation its spatial effect is now limited. It interprets the philosophy of Nicholas Roerich as the motto of the assemblies was 'Unity, Creativity, Beauty'. The composition is a postmodern mixture of various symbols and motifs, dominated by the bell tower in the centre. The shape of the sphere cut out of the concrete planes symbolises the planet, with a bell for each of the seven continents. The 68 bells at ground level come from 68 countries. The Bulgarian bell weighs precisely 1,300 kilograms, referring to the 1,300th anniversary of the Bulgarian State.

Aparthotel Pancharevo

80 Samokovsko Chaussee Street

Boris Enev, Fordewind Architecture

2017

138

SE

The hotel consists of 25 apartment units with covered balconies, two lobbies, a bistro, and a fitness and wellness centre. It is situated in a quiet garden. The three towers, each with its own staircase and elevator, contain the apartment units. Every floor has one or two apartments, each of them orientated in three directions. In order to provide an optimal quality of life, every apartment has its own 20-square-metre loggia overlooking a lake to the north. As the building is situated between the road and the lake, its volume is divided into three parts so that the lake can still be seen between them. The rigorous folded shell façades not only dominate the outside of the building and the spaces between the towers; they also shape the interior of the apartments, thus making every unit unique.

Palace Complex and Vrana Park 139 SE

381 Tsarigradsko Chaussee
Cottage: Georgi Fingov
Palace: Nikola Lazarov
Park: Vasil Georgiev, Konstantin Baykushev, Jules Locheau, Johann Kellerer, Alaricus Delmard, Josef Zollikofer, Anton Kraus, Wilhelm Schacht
1899–1943 (park), 1906 (cottage), 1913 (palace), 1947 (reconstruction)

The complex comprises a villa, a palace, a kitchen, and a linking gallery, in a 19th century landscape park with a singular dendrological and botanical collection. Construction work started in 1899, when the property, known since the 15th century by the name 'Chardakliya', was purchased by Prince (later King) Ferdinand I (1861–1948). The name 'Vrana' is supposed to have been given by the prince, because of the great number of crows there. The contemporary layout of the park and the selection of rare types of vegetation are not based on a master plan; instead they were organically assembled over a period of 44 years under the personal direction of kings Ferdinand I and Boris III. The residential section was constructed in a relatively short period of time. The villa is a magnificent combination: a Viennese Secessionist interpretation of the baroque houses in the city of Plovdiv in the early 19th century. The tectonic logic integrates the plan composition and the elevation design in an early modernist manner. The planning concept and the architecture are evidently a solution by the original author, while the interior's comfort is a direct influence of Vienna's Otto Wagner and Josef Hoffmann schools. The delicate Modern image of the interior transfers to the immediate surroundings following the baroque time-space link, also introduced in the houses of Plovdiv. The organic unity combined with the plasticity of the decorative elements makes the complex one of the highlights of Bulgarian architecture of the time. The romanticist influences can also be found in the construction of the palace, which took place in 1913. The Secessionist interpretation leads back to the aesthetics of medieval Byzantine architecture and the monastery traditions of the Bulgarian National Revival period in the 18th and 19th centuries. The Middle Ages are reflected in the stone sculpture of the fireside, as well as in some plaster ornaments. Some interior designs were inspired by the Venetian style or Russian Imperial-style, such as the Russian Dining Room in Karelian birch, given as a present by the Russian Emperor Alexander III. French classicism can be identified in the cassette ceilings, enriched with shallow Secession sculpture. The influence of the Secession appears in a number of interior and elevation details. The various stylistic influences are unified by a functional baroque composition. The palace was partially damaged by bombardments during the Second World War and rebuilt in 1947, when it was used by Georgi Dimitrov, prime minister at the time. It later served as a representative governmental residence.

Southern Zone

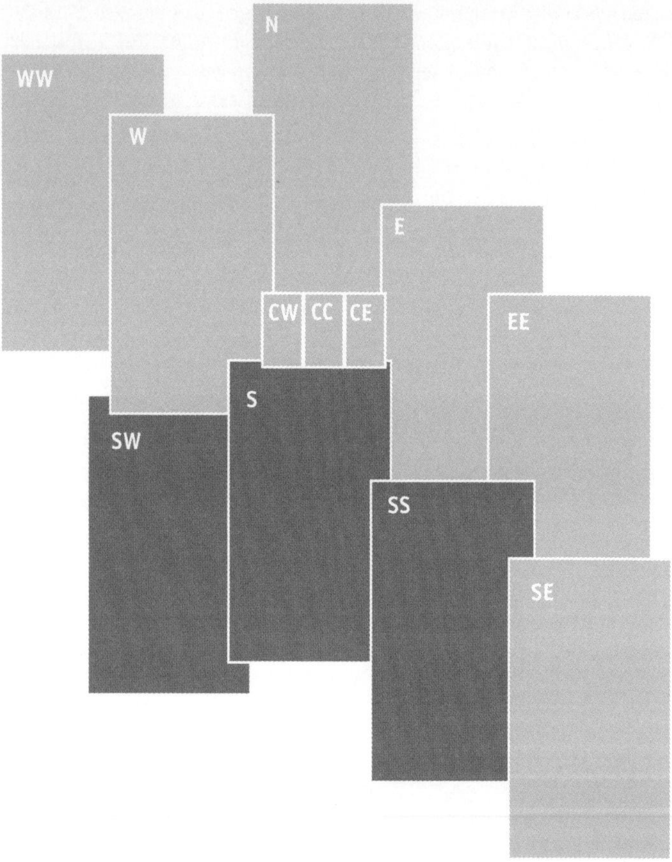

Maps SW, SS, S

The southern territories of Sofia, which are associated with Lozenets Hill, are located at a short distance from the main international and regional roads. The area developed in the context of the connection between the city and Vitosha Mountain since Antiquity and has preserved its meaning as a spiritual and recreational place over the centuries. Even today, the city and the mountain are considered to be in union. Ferdinand Ritter von Hochstetter's claim that 'Sofia and Vitosha are inseparable' served as an argument for the merging of Sofia and Vitosha into a unified region for the Principality of Bulgaria after the Russian-Turkish Liberation War in 1877–1878. The emanation of the spiritual unity between the two locations was personified by the Bulgarian writer Aleko Konstantinov. The view from Vitosha Boulevard to Lozenets Hill and the mountain has inspired the works of a number of romanticist, symbolist, and contemporary authors. The interpretation of this coexistence has gradually changed, though. Some literature sources from the 17th century describe the southern area as a 'Garden of Eden'. The area was a magnetic place for intellectuals and artists around 1900, when a network of educational facilities was established there. The area was radically transformed in the course of its intensive urbanisation after the 1950s, and became an extension of the compact city centre. In the 1970s high-rise buildings were added to the urban landscape, and these served as a motivation for greater changes to the urban scale in the new millennium.

National Palace of Culture (NDK) and Bulgaria Square

140

S

1 Bulgaria Square

Alexander Barov, Kosto Kostov, Milcho Braynov, Atanas Agura et al

1979–1981

The National Palace of Culture (NDK) is an inseparable part of the large-scale ensemble on Bulgaria Square, which integrates diverse transportation facilities, underground spaces including a metro station, and a square with a garden and several architectural and sculptural compositions. The ensemble was a key element in the development of the southern city centre in the 1970s and 1980s. The area of the former military barracks was considered to have potential for an urban transformation as early as the 1960s. After an international competition for an opera house, the outcome of which was not pursued, the idea for a multifunctional public and cultural centre was born. The NDK is a multifunctional building for events, congresses and conferences, international forums, concerts, exhibitions, etc. It stands on an area of 18,300 square metres. The gross floor area is an impressive 123,000 square metres of space, organised over eight floors, including three underground levels. The building has 13 event halls with the largest, Hall 1, containing 3,380 seats. The amphitheatre Hall 2 with its 500 seats is mainly used for studio theatre performances. The flat Hall 3 is located above Hall 1 and is used for exhibitions, concerts, and various meetings. All halls are connected with wide foyers, some of which have separate entrances from the surrounding public space. A panorama bar, restaurant, and several coffee shops are linked to the entrances. The multifunctional underground retail and service area has a separate entrance from the public-transport level. The rich presence of visual arts in the architectural concept of the NDK is an important and unique characteristic of the building. The synthesis of architecture and the arts was a typical attempt in Bulgarian architecture of the 1980s. It expresses some basic themes, such as the historic development and the characteristics of Bulgarian culture, as well as the presentation of the diversity of artistic solutions and creative individualities, even if in the context of communist ideology. Dozens of works by prominent artists are exhibited in key locations in the building, among them sculptural figures, reliefs, wall-painting compositions, mosaics and glass-paintings. Space was also reserved for artisanal handcrafts such as tapestry, decorative pottery, wood carving, and metalwork. Georgi Chapkanov's panel *Sun* on the main elevation, Dimitar

Boykov's sculpture *Homeland* in the main foyer, and the wall paintings by Dechko Uzunov, Hristo Stefanov, Yoan Leviev, and Svetlin Russev are of special interest. The NDK ensemble plays an important role in Sofia's urban image. The synthesis of architecture, landscape design, and the arts was a model for the representative style of architecture in the late 1970s and the 1980s. It expressed the revival of an ensemble driven by thinking in the spirit of monumentality and classicism. As a rule, the arts followed the Modern Movement, but they nevertheless showed a strong link to national traditions. The ensemble was also indicative of construction possibilities during the late socialist period. That blend of principles of expression that stem from different architectural languages – the classical symmetry found in modernist elements and features such as the cantilevered silhouette – not only gives the building its contradictory and postmodern appearance, it also lends it relevance to its temporal and local context.

Cooperative apartment building

141

S

28 Patriarch Evtimiy Boulevard
Vasko Vassilev
1935

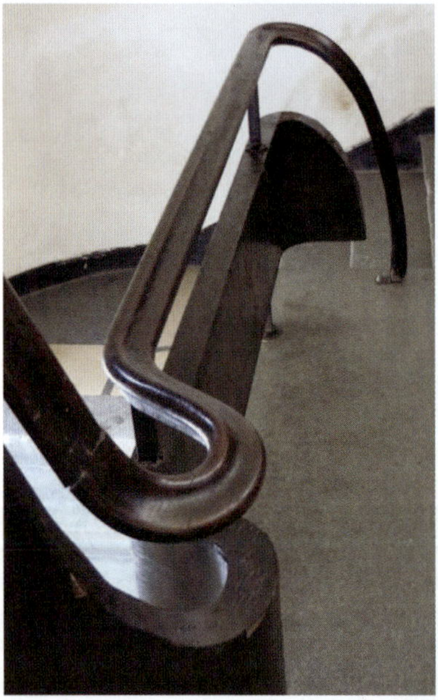

This edifice is one of Vasko Vassilev's early projects and shows his ideas of how to treat the façade of an apartment building in a row: the symmetrical composition, the terrace on the upper floor, the finishing element at the top of the façade, the clear and simple detail, the general rigorous image. Constructed during a period when cantilevered elements towards the street were prohibited, the building has a flat façade. However, Vassilev managed to turn it into a sober composition with a few features. The top floor is set inwards, creating a second plan, while the middle part of the façade is accentuated by both the minimal balcony on the top level and the discrete change of materials. The windows are incorporated into a common frame on each level and form horizontal bands. The details are precise, even minimalist. The interior design is much more sophisticated; the details of the staircases, the railings, and the apartment doors are carefully thought out.

Private house →

142

S

51 6th September Street
Svetoslav Goranov, Panteley Tsvetkov. Restoration and reconstruction: Krasimir Valkov, Gergana Saralieva
1929, 2008 (restoration)

Located in a row of various types of urban villas, the building stands out in its heterogeneous surroundings through its massive *avant-corps* in the south-western corner. The horizontal window-strips play an important role in the modernist structuring of the volume. The elevation's decoration is reduced to simple window frames and exposed clinker brickwork. The impressive original frieze of decorative pointed arches in clinker gives the building a finished look. The interior elements – the fireplaces, the masonry stoves, the large wooden gates, the massive wooden interior doors, the original double-glazed windows – were preserved and partly refurbished. The building is one of the few good examples of Romantic Expressionism in Bulgarian architecture during the interwar period.

Madara Public Baths and Swimming Pool ↓

143

S

21 Praga Boulevard/
Pencho Slaveykov Boulevard
Angel Damyanov
1946

The implementation of public services for sports, hygiene, and healthcare was one of the political programmes of the first years of Communist rule. The building can be surveyed as a result of the interaction between different fields. It was constructed just after the Second World War, during early Communist rule, and thus bridges two different epochs. The spatial structure of the baths is designed within a modernist tradition, but its courtyard composition refers to Classical prototypes, and the whole building is dressed in a somewhat National Romanticist style with Byzantine overtones. These features, along with the use of traditional stone for cladding, place the building in the category of a local version of post-war critical regionalism. At present, the edifice functions as a recreation, fitness, and sports facility with a covered swimming pool.

Cooperative apartment building →

144

S

38 Vasil Levski Boulevard
Attributed to Angel Momov
1928

Although located on a large boulevard, the building is free-standing. Its purist cubical form is enriched by triangular oriel windows. The façade is horizontally articulated by alternating bands of colour and plasterwork. The detail on the stucco is executed with high degree of precision. The flat roof, the meticulous stripes, and the simplistic expression form a straightforward modernist language. The building is one of the most unconventional works from the interwar period in Sofia and resembles the façade experimentation typical for the expressiveness of art deco. The classicist nuances are recognisable in the tripartite articulation of the façade and also in the attic floor. The definitive geometry of the polygonal volume at the back of the building evokes some constructivist associations.

Polish Embassy ↓

145

S

46 Khan Krum Street
Bohdan Pniewski
1938

The building was designed for a competition held in Poland in 1928. Its Polish creator, Bohdan Pniewski, was a notorious modernist architect of the era, known for designing important public and administrative buildings and luxurious private houses. His modernist outlook was more grounded in aesthetics than in a social or technological approach. In his projects he often mixed a modernist language with historical or regional references. The embassy building has a simple layout yet is also elaborate. Although it is not very big, it makes a distinct impression compared to the other residential buildings in the area. The entrance façade towards Khan Krum Street has a modernist, monumental character. The upper cantilevered floor is balanced by the oval staircase, which, reminiscent of a medieval tower, marks the entrance of the building. The details are refined; the stone cladding is sophisticated and carefully worked out. The building has a different appearance towards the garden. On the first level the representative spaces are linked directly to the park area in front, while on the second level there is a large loggia.

Cooperative apartment building ↓

146

S

58 Vasil Levski Boulevard

Hristo Berberov

1937

This monolithic residential structure with varying heights stands at the point where Vasil Levski Boulevard crosses a smaller street. The curve of the boulevard gives visibility to the corner from a great distance away, and this fact determined the concept. Instead of developing a façade composition, the architect designed a volumetric one. The building consists of two main elements: a corner cuboid with a delicate frame around it. The solidity is emphasised by the evenly distributed square windows. Although they are in the same plane, the volumes can be easily read. The frame is formed by the slim verticals in front of the staircase glazing and the narrow slit under the roof slab. The composition is minimalistic. Logically, the roof is flat. The absolute lack of ornament highlights the main concept and the purist beauty of the stereometric forms.

Apartment building ↑

147

S

37 Evlogi and Hristo Georgievi Boulevard

Vasko Vassilev

1943

Designed in the early 1940s, the building showcases the approaches Vasko Vassilev implemented in his apartment buildings from the late 1930s and the 1940s. As the edifice is located on the corner of Evlogi and Hristo Georgievi Boulevard and a smaller road, the architect took the opportunity to create an elaborate feature using the meeting point of the two streets. This corner feature is formed of a stack of recessed loggias with large, flat, convexly curved windows, all unified by a slim column running through them. The pergola above the terrace on the top floor ends with a semi-circular protruding edge – a particularly impressive feature. The motif of the convex-curved windows is repeated on the façade along the smaller road, in a similar way to that of Vassilev's apartment building on William Gladstone Street (see 035).

Patriarch Evtimiy Square (Popa) ↓

148

S

Patriarch Evtimiy Boulevard/
Vasil Levski Boulevard/
Graf Ignatiev Street

Patriarch Evtimiy Monument ↓

Sculptor: Marko Markov; 1937

Family residence ↓

2 Patriarch Evtimiy Boulevard
Petko Momchilov; 1899

'Popa', is a crucial node in Sofia city centre. It is a busy square with many corners and principal axes visible from long distances away, as well as a common meeting spot for the people of Sofia. To use Louis Kahn's notion, it is a 'place to go from'. The focal point is the Monument to Patriarch Evtimiy , called Popa ('the priest'), erected in memory of Saint Euthymius of Tarnovo (1317–1402), the Patriarch of Bulgaria from 1375 to 1393. He was the last head of the Bulgarian Orthodox Church in the Second Bulgarian Kingdom (1185–1396), before it came under Ottoman rule. Euthymius, who led the defence of the capital Veliko Tarnovo, is regarded as one of the most important figures of medieval Bulgaria. He initiated spelling and linguistic reforms of the Bulgarian language and led the Tarnovo Literary School. The bronze statue was put up after a competition in 1936. Behind the statue stands Notary House, a building which was constructed in a neo-Renaissance style as a single-family residence and was used as the German Embassy during the Second World War.

The Red House - Andrey Nikolov Centre for Culture and Debate ↘

149

S

15 Lyuben Karavelov Street
Ivan Vasilyov with the participation of Andrey Nikolov.
Restoration and adaptation: Ivaylo Petkov, Lyuben Boyadzhiev, Tsvetan Tsinzev
1928, 2002 (restoration)

Although the house was designed by the architect Ivan Vasilyov, it showcases the ideas of its owner – the sculptor Andrey Nikolov. Having spent 13 years in Rome, the artist was inspired by Italian architecture and created a building influenced by the artistic impulses born from the peculiar marriage between classicist and

modernist trends in European architecture of the time. Along with the usual living spaces, the house incorporates an atelier and workshops. At present the large space of the master's workshop is used as an exhibition and performance centre. All these elements create a spatial labyrinth, connected through stairs and terraces. The building has an emblematic image: the cubic volume of the atelier dominates the foreground, partly concealing the rest of the building. The forms are clear and enriched with Classical details such as the entrance, the rustication, the arched windows. In this building, these aspects of Classical architecture are used symbolically rather than as decorative elements.

Cooperative apartment building →

150

S

66 Vasil Levski Boulevard

Radoslav Radoslavov, Konstantin Dzhangozov

1940

This residential building has a sober, entirely modernist expression. One can read the whole spatial composition in its only façade. Squeezed between its neighbours in a row of buildings, it explores the concepts of empty and full – the balance between the materiality of the cantilever and the balconies and the emptiness created by the recessed back plan. The large frame enclosing the entire façade separates it from the row and gives it a clear and straightforward articulation. As a second line of thought, the horizontality of the long spans of the parapets and windows stands in contrast to the verticality of the recessed staircase. The details are minimal but eloquent: the plain plaster façade is enriched by the linear window frames and the slits in the parapets. Originally, the roof was not visible from the street and the building had a horizontal finish; the glazed superstructure was added later.

Cooperative apartment building

151

S

12 Patriarch Evtimiy Boulevard
Vasko Vassilev
ca. 1939

This building, where Vasko Vassilev's own apartment is located, showcases the architect's mature concept for the façade layout of a row building. The continuous spans of the wall mark the façade plane, which is interrupted by the concavely and convexly curved windows. The round corner columns through the loggias have both a constructive and an expressive role. They express the symbolic axis around which the substance of the building pivots. The proportions of the columns seem a bit sturdy, but this fact is quite skilfully counteracted by the elegant detachment between the wall and the beam. The perfectly symmetrical composition gives the façade a rigorous look, yet the continuous windows and the glazing in the middle relieve some of the visual weight. The thin cornice projects outwards from the façade plane and completes the composition.

Faculty of Agronomy and Institute of Agriculture

152

S

8 Dragan Tsankov Boulevard
Georgi Ovcharov
1936

The complex comprises two separate objects: the main building of the Faculty of Agronomy, which faces Dragan Tsankov Boulevard to the north-east, and the secondary building of the Institute of Agriculture, located behind it, and accessible from Hristo Smirnenski Boulevard. The faculty building follows a classical symmetrical organisation with the main entrance and the assembly hall located in the centre. The cylindrical volume of the assembly hall is clearly articulated with its flat pilasters structure, finishing with a massive wall with blind arches in it. The assembly hall is impressive, with the exaggerated verticality of its windows and the pointed Gothic arches of the public spaces. Over all the façades there are more than ten different types of window openings varying in size and shape. The edifice of the Institute of Agriculture maintains the character and the language of the faculty building, although it is designed with less monumentality and with more flexibility of the public spaces. The two parts of the complex share sophisticated brickwork detailing in both the exterior and interior spaces. The large, gently curved brick wall surfaces relate the building to Northern European examples

of expressionist, late classicist, and early art deco – in particular to Stockholm Public Library, which was designed by Gunnar Asplund and was completed the same year the design for the faculty was started. Currently the buildings have a different use: part of the complex has been converted to fulfil the needs of Sofia City Court, with the large lecture rooms used for court sessions.

Simon apartment building 153 S

12–16 Dragan Tsankov Boulevard
Atanas Panov, Lorita Panova, LP Group
2004

The building is located in one of the most attractive residential areas in Sofia, in close proximity to the Borisova Gradina park. It includes a number of high-end apartments which start from the third floor, while the ground floor and mezzanine are reserved for office and retail space. Each of the two parts of the building – the lower pedestal with the offices and the higher residential volume – are concluded with a pergola motif at the top. The ceramic cladding of the façades replicates the nearby Faculty of Agriculture by Georgi Ovcharov, a masterpiece from the 1930s. The clear lines of the silhouette and the simple volumes of the otherwise complex building shape add to the simple monumentality of the edifice.

University of Architecture, Civil Engineering and Geodesy (UACEG) 154 S

1 Hristo Smirnenski Boulevard
Angel Delibashev, Ivan Popov, Milko Angelov, Chavdar Angelov. Reliefs: Valentin Starchev
1974

The beginning of the 1970s was characterised by a number of competitions for university campuses. This university complex is one of the most prominent

examples. Situated in the south-eastern part of the city centre, it forms an ensemble with the old buildings of the UACEG and the High School for Construction Technology. The new extension from the 1970s is oriented along the boulevard, with the main entrance situated in the end furthest from the existing building. It comprises a three-floor lower section and two high-rises at the back of the plot. The main foyer, the canteen, the library, the administration offices, and the larger lecture halls surround the inner court, which remains unused today. A secondary entrance faces the green area to the south. The teaching halls are organised in the two towers, one of 10 and one of 12 floors. The recessed terraces between the cantilevered volumes supply a sculptural dynamic to the towers. The complex acts a vertical accent in the silhouette of the city. The lecture halls protruding towards the boulevard are rhythmically arranged. Their front sides are decorated with geometric reliefs, abstractly presenting the construction process.

Bulgarian National Radio ↑

155

S

4 Dragan Tsankov Boulevard
Georgi Stoilov
1970

The old building for Radio Sofia from 1942 contained a hall with 400 seats. The façade design with exaggerated pilasters followed the principles of German rational classicism. The new building was erected to the north of the old one, and both were connected with a passage on the second floor. The new building has a unique steel-skeleton structure with curtain-wall surfaces and aluminium windows. The cantilevered storey-volumes define the specific compact silhouette of an upside-down pyramid which carries its own specific representativeness and monumentality.

Sofia Spiritual Seminary and St Ivan Rilski Church →

156

S

2 Velchova Zavera Square
Friedrich Grünanger.
Reconstruction: Genko Popov.
Iconostasis: Avram Avramov, Petar Yosifov
1904, 1938 (reconstruction),
1951 (interior changes),
1952 (iconostasis)

The foundation stone of the Bulgarian Orthodox Church's main school was laid in 1902 and lessons started in the following years. The formation of the complex began with the main building and the church, and then continued over a period of 35 years. The boarding school was used as a military hospital during the First World War. In the 1920s the buildings also accommodated the Faculty of Agronomy of Sofia University. Additional school and service buildings, as well as the south-western part of the main building, were completed at the same time. The decorated fence wall and the Presveta Bogoroditsa Portalnitsa Chapel next to the entrance were finished in 1927. Additional requirements led to an extension of the church to the east. During the Second World War the buildings housed the headquarters of the Soviet Army and were damaged by the air raids. Afterwards, the complex was converted into the Palace of the Pioneers, and then was returned to the Church in 1990. The architecture is a Romantic interpretation of local medieval traditions and the trends during the National Revival period. The Byzantine influence is obvious in the design of the elevations, as well as in the central, cross-dome church St Ivan Rilski and the Venetian arches introduced in the design of the iconostasis. The original Secessionist icons of the iconostasis were replaced on canonical grounds with new ones in the spirit of the Byzantine tradition at the beginning of the 21st century.

View along Cherni Vrah Boulevard towards Vitosha Mountain
with the Hilton Hotel (157) on the right-hand side

157

Hilton Hotel

157

S

1 Bulgaria Boulevard
Ricardo Bofill Taller de Arquitectura Paris, Atelier IRA. Local architects: Lozan Lozanov, Atanas Panov
2001

In 1994, following a decree by Sofia Municipal Council, a Bulgarian-French company was founded for the design, construction, and maintenance of a five-star hotel located in South Park, behind the National Palace of Culture. The company invited Ricardo Bofill Taller de Arquitectura Paris to design a hotel in co-operation with a Bulgarian partner, Atelier IRA. In 1995 the project for an 18-storey building with an atrium was approved. The design encountered serious criticism with regard to its location and connection to the park, its strict symmetry, its stark exterior, and especially its height, which would have blocked views towards Vitosha Mountain. As a result, the project was revised by decreasing the overall height of the building by almost half and seriously altering its original layout. The new project was submitted in 1998 and three years later the hotel was completed. The building consists of two distinct volumes joined by a communication core and situated as an open book facing Bulgaria Boulevard. Both volumes are clad in white stone with regularly spread identical small openings, creating a deliberate visual contrast to the glass-covered entrance atrium. The hotel is designed around a self-inflicted post-modern axis of symmetry, which opens it to the city, the National Palace of Culture, and the busy streets nearby, but makes no connection to the surrounding park area.

National Finance and Business High School (former Sofia High School of Commerce for Boys)

158

S

1 Rozova Dolina Street

Michail Pushkarov. Sculpture: Kiril Shivarov

1930

The all-male secondary school was founded by the Bulgarian Chamber of Commerce and Industry in 1913. The building's layout follows the irregular U-shape defined by the surrounding streets. The fronts are structured by the rhythm of the large stone-framed windows. A recessed clock-tower in the north-western corner marks the main entrance. The wider pavement, the sculpturally framed doors and windows, the diminishing windows in the upper levels, and the figure of Hermes, the Greek god of trade, all add to the expressiveness of the entrance. In contrast, the other corner is curved and plays a secondary role. The overall architecture expresses a classicist quietness. The sculptured entrance shape shows the mixed influences of eclecticism and romanticism. With regard to the interior, the foyers and staircase are worthy of note.

Remains of an Ottoman religious object (mihrab wall)

159

S

1 Stara Stena Street

16th century

Although widely known by Sofia's citizens as the 'Roman Wall', these remains are in fact part of the south-eastern wall of a structure from the Ottoman period. There are several hypotheses on the intended purpose of the object, with the most probable being a mausoleum (*türbe*). The central building had a square plan covered with a dome. It was a part of a Muslim cemetery, the traces of which were present until the beginning of the 20th century. Some characteristic architectural features of the wall are the specific Byzantine *Opus reticulatum* (reticulated work), where stones are framed by bricks from its four sides, and the cornice ornamentation in 'wolf's tooth' brick-bond, where bricks are rotated at a 45-degree angle. The mihrab has been preserved. This niche was used to orient prayers along the sacral vector pointing in the direction of Mecca. Nowadays the remains have turned into an important landmark for the site, as they are in the middle of a farmers' market named the 'Roman Wall'. It is an active social area opposite the University of Architecture, Civil Engineering and Geodesy.

122nd Elementary School – Nikolay Liliev ↑

160

S

2 Prezviter Kozma Street
Vladimir Romenski, Anastas Perfanov
1964

The building stands on a steep plot next to Cherni Vrah Boulevard. It is an example of the modernist trend that developed in Bulgarian school architecture after the mid-1950s. It presents an alternative to the common at the time model of single-volume, classicist educational blocks with rooms around a central corridor. The building is masterfully landscaped in the complicated terrain and has a lavish courtyard.

Orbita Hotel (former youth complex) ↓

161

S

31 Cherni Vrah Boulevard (between James Bourchier Boulevard, Cherni Vrah Boulevard, and Petar Stanchev Street)
Georgi Stoilov, Lyudmil Kazaski, Teofan Nikiforov. Structural engineer: Blagoy Anastasov
1974

The Orbita ensemble was once a youth recreational complex that was part of a network of similar structures, spread throughout Bulgaria. Located on top of Lozenets Hill, it offers panoramic views over Sofia, along with the Balkan

Mountain Range to the north and Vitosha Mountain to the south. It was deliberately designed as a low, five-storey volume in order not to disturb the vistas, and its shape responds to the configuration of the surrounding streets. The main entrance is situated to the south. The expressiveness of the horizontal façade is achieved through the chequer pattern of windows and solid parts. The geometric dynamic is enhanced by the play of light and shadows and the contrast between the white mosaic and the brown plaster. In recent years the mosaic panel by Apostol Ruskov on the eastern blind wall was lost because of new additions to the building.

Lozenets apartment building 162

S

28 Dimitar Hadzhikotsev Street
AEDES Studio/Plamen Bratkov, Rossitsa Bratkova
2010

A rectangular grid of white stone planes and individual 'cell' apartments forms the basis for this housing block. Within the grid cells, the architects installed 'showcases' – interfaces between the inside and outside spaces – which bring in the maximum amount of light from the narrow streets. They added sliding screens to allow the inhabitants to regulate the intensity of light indoors and to protect against overheating, while also changing the appearance of the building itself. The perforation on these wooden panels is consciously chaotic, and does not conform to a regular geometric pattern, in order to generate a play of light in the interior. This effect has a double purpose: during the day the sun's rays enter the interior, whereas in the evening the building casts rays of light above the street. The intimacy of the home is also preserved on the terraces, which can be fully hidden from view. The staircase has a dramatic design, with a folding pattern on the underside of the stairs. At basement level, there is an office. In front of this is a semi-private and semi-public space – an area of transition. All of the façade engineering, sliding mechanisms, and details were custom developed by Bulgarian companies for the building.

Sofia Arsenal – Museum for Contemporary Art

163

S

2 Cherni Vrah Boulevard
Kadinov Bros Agency for Architecture/Boyko Kadinov
2011

The old Sofia Arsenal complex, built from 1882 to 1916, is an architectural heritage monument of local importance. It is situated in a park behind the Sofia Hilton Hotel and near the National Palace of Culture. The project for the Museum for Contemporary Art adapted the space of the historic building to the programme for art exhibitions, presentations, and debates. A shell made from 11 tonnes of glass packages part of the building. This transparent shell, which hangs from a stainless-steel frame and steel cables, is designed to be an interface between the historical image and the space of the park. The glass stairs and membrane transform the façade into an interactive space, transforming the museum itself into an installation that one can experience as a piece of art. The building bridges time in a single location and juxtaposes materials and styles. The project was implemented under the Cultural Heritage and Contemporary Arts Programme, financed through the European Economic Area Financial Mechanism.

Earth and Man National Museum (former Great Workshop Building of the Sofia Artillery Arsenal)

164

S

4 Cherni Vrah Boulevard

Unknown Austrian architect.
Reconstruction: Hristo Ganchev and team.
Exposition arrangement: Ivan Radev.
Wall paintings: Teofan Sokerov

1900, 1987

Constructed around 1882, this large former workshop is one of the three preserved buildings of the Sofia Arsenal complex. Its elevations are designed in a rationalised art-nouveau style, complying with the function and the structure. The building was the first reinforced concrete frame construction with ribbed covering in Bulgaria. It is an early example of the reinforced concrete structural system developed by the French engineer François Hennebique in 1892. The frame structure of beams and columns creates an imposing three-nave space with a gallery. The functional skylights located above the central nave support the sculptural appearance of the constructive elements. The building is today part of South Park, which was proposed in Adolf Mussmann's urban plan as early as 1938. The museum was established in 1986. It has over 31,000 exhibits, and offers an impressive exposition of giant crystals and minerals donated by 912 collectors from Bulgaria and abroad. The space and the architecture of the Great Workshop Building were preserved in the course of its reconstruction and contain the permanent exhibition. The scientific and administrative offices are located to the west, facing South Park. That part was completely refurbished as a postmodern interpretation of the main building. The architecture reflects the significance of the cultural institution and the scale of the park. The colour solution positions the large building volume very delicately, both within the park and against the silhouette of Vitosha Mountain.

Aries Offices

165

S

Cherni Vrah Blvd/Viskiar Street
LP Group/Atanas Panov, Lorita Panova
2008

The area of Lozenets, with its tree-lined streets, has become a desirable location for the offices of various types of companies. This has led to the transformation of the district into a highly eclectic mixture of building types, competing in peculiarity. In this context, the architects opted for overall simplicity and a modest rectangular design as a strategy to attract attention. The basic concept of the design was to delineate the edgy silhouette with a simple element, namely the filigree stone grid, which encloses and links the volumes, as defined by the urban master plan. That led to the creation of an unconventional office building which refuses to be anything more than an office building in the context of a complex urban fabric, and denies the use of features such as increased height, curvilinear silhouettes, or other instruments of individualisation. The abstract arrangement of the granite stone cladding covers the glass curtain-wall and provides sustainability.

Red Apple Apartments

166

S

24 Byala Cherkva Street
AEDES Studio/Plamen Bratkov, Rossitsa Bratkova
2012

This building, which contains 61 unique apartments, is located on the edge of South Park, between the two entrances to the green space. The architects – Plamen Bratkov, Rossitsa Bratkova, and their firm AEDES Studio – designed a hybrid structure between a multistory apartment building and a factory, which refers to the typology of the industrial loft adapted for dwelling. This 'residential factory' demanded a brick-wall aesthetic, masterfully arranged in the Flemish bond brickwork. Since raising the height of the single apartments was not considered a viable economic solution from the developer's point of view, the architects compromised on their initial concept by increasing the heights of some of the living rooms – this is visible from outside as oversized double-height windows. These elements bring an almost public scale to the building's expression. The loft scale, the red-brick surfaces, and the black iron mesh-work of the balconies give the project

a 'Manhattan-esque' flavour, connecting the Red Apple to the Big Apple. The apartments are grouped in clusters within the contour of the plan, around the exaggerated space of the vertical atrium in the core of the building. An inner space but at the same time left uncovered for ventilation, the atrium embodies the duality intrinsic to the entire design of the Red Apple Apartments.

Bulgaria Square/South Park

167

S

Open spaces: Atanas Agura, Valentina Atanassova. Underground spaces: Atanas Agura, Stanislav Konstantinov, Mariana Stoichkova. Artist: Ivan Radev; 1981. Open-air theatre: Todor Boulev; 2010.

The first sector of South Park integrates the National Palace of Culture (NDK), diverse transportation facilities, underground spaces, and several sculptural compositions. Its realisation was the most significant urban transformation for the organisation of public spaces after the Second World War. Bulgaria Square directed the orientation of the city centre to South Park and Vitosha Mountain. It is organised along a strong north–south axis, which leads to the main entrance of the NDK. Water basins with fountains run along the axis, emphasising the significance of the building. The composition has some additional components, such as the picturesque children's playground carved into the terrain. Part of the landscape was transformed into an open-air theatre. Another component is the Memorial to the Victims of Communism from 1944 to 1989, designed by Dimitar Krastev and Ivan Smolyanov. It combines a small chapel, a memorial wall with the names of the victims, and an authentic stone-carved crest from the 18th century. The space in front of the Palace of Culture is organised over two levels. The underground level, which links to the public transportation stations, is the compositional centre of the second-main entrance to the palace. The two levels are vertically connected through an octagonal court space with a water fountain. The underground spaces surrounding the palace contain garages and service facilities. As an area for entertainment and recreation, Bulgaria Square is of a importance for the city's identity. The 1,300 Years of Bulgaria Monument, which was erected on the occasion of the 1,300th anniversary of the Bulgarian State and was designed by the sculptor Valentin Starchev and the architect Alexander Braynov, was removed in 2017 in spite of public protests.

South Park's second sector and largest component is a 200-hectare green wedge that stretches from Vitosha Mountain to Sofia city centre. The wedge idea was first developed by Adolf Mussmann in 1938 in his urban development plan for Sofia. The layout of the green area follows the

English landscape garden, with its picturesque network of alleys oriented to four entrances, and a combination of meadows and green spaces. The main entrance in the north is an axial extension of Vitosha Boulevard. Some characteristic features of the park are the Perlovska River and a system of natural and artificial water basins. To the east the steep slopes of Lozenets Hill extend into the park. The natural effect is completed by some artificial hills next to the western outlines, which serve as noise protection from the boulevard.

Park Hotel Moskva

168

S

25 Nezabravka Street
Alexander Belokapov
1974

The project was the result of an architectural competition for prestigious hotels in Sofia, Burgas, and Russe, announced in 1964. The hotel's status is also clear from its location on one of Sofia's main boulevards and next to the Borisova Gradina park. All of the guest rooms have panoramic vistas over the city, the park, and Vitosha Mountain. The high-rise volume is individualised through a trapezoid base form and vertical structural elements that protrude from the glass façade. The low part of the hotel contains conference halls, a restaurant, a winter garden, a bar, and other rooms – all connected by a grand foyer. A panorama restaurant is situated on the top floor.

Hotel Marinela (former Hotel Vitosha)

169

S

100 James Bourchier Boulevard
Kisho Kurokawa, Kohatsu, Shibata. Sculpture: Olya Kolcheva, Zdravko Mavrodiev, Ana Tuszusova, Georgi Chapkanov
1978

This five-star hotel is situated on an area of 30,000 square metres and has 442 guest rooms. It was the first building in Eastern Europe by the world-renowned Japanese architect Kisho Kurokawa (1934–2007). Although Kurokawa was a protagonist of metabolism, an incredibly complex and innovative approach to design, in the case of this hotel, a pragmatic design approach prevailed, and the project responded to a common combination for the time: a high-rise building and a low service platform containing periphery facilities. With its 24 floors, the hotel is a main feature in the skyline of Sofia. The tall building was composed with two specific features: ventilation ducts installed on the façade, and corner bay-windows that protrude from the main volume, reminiscent of 'rustic' stone decoration, in the spirit of the postmodern concealed historicism that prevailed at the time. The low horizontal platform was set in a dialogue with the scale of the surrounding buildings. The lavish ground floor lends prestige to the composition with its main entrance, and the inner courtyard partly opens to the boulevard. The courtyard was designed as an elaborate Japanese garden with a tea pavilion set in the artificial pond, and thus it created a world in itself. This was modelled on a 400-year-old Japanese garden in Tokyo. Visitors pass along the organic outline of the courtyard to restaurants, exposition rooms, and conference halls. The design of the ground floor offers manifold impressions. Works by Bulgarian artists contribute to the dominant Japanese motifs and evoke the artistic atmosphere in Sofia in the late 1970s. Unfortunately, both the spirit of the initial design and the Japanese garden suffered extensively under the interventions carried out by the new owners of the building.

VG
Hotel Marinela

Museum of Socialist Art ↑↘ 170 SS

7 Lachezar Stanchev Street
Curator: Nikolay Ushtavaliyski
2011

The Museum of Socialist Art is a subsidiary of the National Art Gallery and is the first exhibition space and museum institution dedicated exclusively to artworks from Bulgaria's socialist period (1944–1989). It is located in an existing building – a property belonging to the Bulgarian Ministry of Culture – which underwent extensive reconstruction works in 2011. At present the museum's collection includes a sculpture park with 77 works, an exhibition hall with an area of 550 square metres, and a multimedia hall for screening documentaries. The open-air exhibition collects brass, stone, and concrete sculptures which once decorated public places in Sofia and other Bulgarian cities. Among the communist leaders portrayed, one may recognise local and international figures like Lenin, Stalin, Georgi Dimitrov, and others. The red star made of custom-produced ruby glass is one of the exhibition's more conspicuous artefacts. From 1954 until 1989, it was installed at the top of the spire of Party House (see 019).

Sopharma and Litex Towers → 171 SS

5 Lachezar Stanchev Street,
1797 Iztok Housing Complex
Dimitar Paskalev, Architektonika Studio; 2011

The Sopharma and Litex Business Towers complex is located in a developing part of Sofia and is surrounded by a park and sports grounds. It includes three office

towers – two for Sopharma and one for Litex – placed on top of a large two-storey-high shopping centre that serves the offices, but also used by the inhabitants of the nearby residential area. The complex has an ambitious mixed-use programme, and a high standard of sustainability, including green certifications. The crystal-glass double-skin façade with its integrated retro-optical shading provides comfortable defused light and at the same time huge energy savings, in comparison with conventional selective glass façades. The dynamic behaviour of the building's skin depends on the automation algorithms, and so the exterior impression changes according to the environmental conditions. The complex became Green Building of the Year in a national competition in 2011.

Interpred – World Trade Center Sofia

172

S

36 Dragan Tsankov Boulevard
Vladimir Romenski, Ivan Yankov, Esteyco Madrid; 1986

This building is located in an area that since the 1960s has developed as a zone for representative and economic activities, and embassies. The building is set back from the line of the street and has an open square in front of its pyramid-shaped covered atrium. The height difference and interstice between the office blocks adds a dramatic expression to the solidly structured architecture. The functional homogeneity prompted the architects to pack the edifice in a technological and functional glass-and-steel curtain wall. The simplistic elevation permits a sculptural solution with geometrical clarity. The ground level is accessible through the covered entrance plaza of the atrium. With its glass monumentality in a late-modernist language, the building has preserved its remarkable urban presence, despite the many new high-rise buildings in the area.

Lyubata apartment building

173

S

12 Lyubata Street
AEDES Studio/Plamen Bratkov, Rossitsa Bratkova
2012

Contrary to most of the surrounding structures in the Lozenets district – a location that was chaotically overbuilt during the 1990s – this apartment building follows a vernacular barn-building tradition. It comprises a 'heavy' stone ground floor and a 'light' wooden volume on top. In order to decrease the weightiness of the wooden volume and to strengthen the building's individual aesthetic, the architects divided the volume into four different-sized sections. These sections are separated by strips of glass in sections set back from the wooden façade. Seen from the street, the building gives the viewer the impression that it is a row of houses. As the ground floor sits back underneath the wooden volumes, it creates the sense that the volumes are levitating above the stone – an effect that is most evident at night when the glass stripe above the ground floor is lit up.

Muzeiko Children's Museum
3 Prof. Boyan Kamenov Street
LHSA+DP, A&A Architects
2015

174
SS

Completed in 2015, Muzeiko is the first children's museum in Bulgaria and the largest such institution in South-eastern Europe. The project was funded by a private foundation and is currently the largest non-governmental project in the field of education and culture in Bulgaria. To create the contemporary scientific and educational children's centre, the US practice LHSA+DP, working together with the Bulgarian firm A&A, reconstructed and refurbished an abandoned building. Several thematic exhibitions related to culture, history, ecology, science, and technology are installed in Muzeiko. The exhibits are divided into three themes – the past, the present, and the future – and each is distributed over one of the three floors of the 3,250-square-metre building. The exhibits were designed and produced for Muzeiko by an international team. Interactive features are spread throughout the site and include a green roof with a climbing wall. The main volume is broken up by three sculptural volumes based on the theme 'little mountains'. These reference Bulgaria's topography through their shapes, and highlight the country's craft traditions with their colours, patterns, and textures.

Bellissimo Business Centre
102 Bulgaria Boulevard
Elite Architecture Studio, Kalin Dikov. Structural and mechanical engineering: Ircon, Mikhail Tsankov
2006

175
SW

The Bellissimo Business Centre is a high-end office building on Bulgaria Boulevard, one of Sofia's busiest boulevards, near the intersection with the city's ring road. It is made up of three volumes – of six, nine and twelve floors – interlinked in a dynamic composition that counterposes the silhouette of Vitosha Mountain. The interplay of the reflections of the building in its own curvilinear glass surfaces brings an intricate richness to its expression. The structure's two parts are connected as one spatial organism through their inner spaces and with the reception and lobby on the ground floor. The lobby is configured as a glass atrium reaching the seventh floor. Besides offices, the Centre also includes other functions such as a restaurant and cafe, retail space, and business apartments. It was constructed from 2004 to 2006, and in 2006 the *Stroitelstvo Gradat* newspaper awarded the business centre the Building of the Year prize in their national competition.

A3 – Advanced Architecture Apartments →

176

SW

112 Bulgaria Boulevard
STARH/Svetoslav Stanislavov
2017

Two starting points – Vitosha Mountain and the city of Sofia – set the overall architectural concept for this residential building, as it is located near the edge of the city, where the mountain begins. Developed from 2015 to 2017 and situated in one of the fastest developing areas of Sofia, A3 Advanced Architecture Apartments is designed to be contemporary and contextual. The building volume is divided into five blocks, which are linked in a common ensemble. The complex creates the impression of a cut-through section of an organic multicellular structure, where each cell volume is outlined with a soft and elegant skin. Nevertheless, the floor plans are laid out in rectangular and rational forms. All 160 apartment units are fully glazed to the east. The ground floor contains standard service and commercial facilities such as shopping areas. The façade is composed of two materials: glass (two types) and glass-fibre-reinforced concrete.

Bulgaria Mall ←→

177

SW

69 Bulgaria Boulevard
Milena Nanova, Plamen Mihaylov, MYS Architects
2012

Situated at the crossroads between Bulgaria and Todor Kableshkov boulevards and developed between 2008 and 2012, the Bulgaria Mall has become part of the modern architectural landscape of this fast-growing area. The 128,000-square-metre mixed-use development consists of a four-storey shopping centre, two office towers, and an underground car park over four floors. Unlike typical mall schemes, the retail areas are organised around a spacious void covered by an impressive glass roof. The 36-metre-high atrium reveals the whole interior of the building and its internal circulation. This lavish scheme makes it easy for visitors to find their way around and offers visibility to any spot inside the mall.

Elena apartments, offices and shops

178

SW

63 Dechko Yordanov Street
Projects GS/Georgi Stanishev
2010

The edifice consists of three parts: a black pedestal, a white prism above it, and a grey metal vault on top. This whole object is inserted among the apartment blocks of a residential complex built in the 1970s and 1980s in the district of Borovo. The horizontal four-storey white-plastered prismatic body contains 30 apartments and stands upon the two-storey black pedestal. The main axis of the tube-like prism is oriented along the 'force lines' of the urban corridor formed by the surrounding residential blocks. The prism is cut on the two short sides to offer visibility towards the park to the east, and to the distant perspective on the opposite side. The vaulted steel structure on top of the prism was designed for large penthouse apartments. The roof vault has a span of 15 metres and houses a unique space, free of structural supports. Its structure is of steel beams and the surface is clad in zinc sheets. The loggias with pergolas are cut into it. The black pedestal platform contains service facilities and retail and office areas, and is clad in glass and ceramic tiles.

Jaclyn residential and office building

179

SW

8 Bulgaria Boulevard
AEDES Studio/Plamen Bratkov, Rossitsa Bratkova; 2007

The building is located in the southern part of Sofia, near a quarter containing high-end single-family homes at the foot of the Vitosha Mountain. Upon assigning the project, the investor specified the theme as 'wood'. Initially the whole façade was lined with wood, but subsequently a less costly solution was found. The first concept image of timber was a pile of wooden planks. The architects wanted to create a hive of family houses, perched on top of each another, to allow the inhabitants to easily recognise their home from outside, as well as inside. The building is composed of multiple volumes that fit into one another. The intention of the design was to include the potential for further development, rather than creating a finite set of elements. The allocation of material and colour across the volume helps to break it up, making it intelligible to the viewer so he or she can grasp it in a single glance. The various graphics that crop up here and there on the boxes contribute to the building's accessibility. They are intended to give the building its own character, rather than simply providing directions.

National History Museum and Boyana Residence (former State Council Representative Complex)

180

SW

Sofia Ring Road/Daskal Stoyan Popandreev Street/
Alexandar Pushkin Boulevard
Alexander Barov, Nadejda Barova, Maria Stoiceva. Landscape: Vasil Mutafchiev
1978

The complex is situated on a large green plot at the foot of the Vitosha Mountain, in the Boyana neighbourhood. The main building was previously the State Council congress centre and has several halls, large foyers, and terraces. It faces the park and the mountain to the south. The symmetrical entrance is oriented towards the city and leads to a grand staircase and the exhibition rooms. The foyer is open to the upper floor and is an enlarged interpretation of a typical space model for 19th-century Bulgarian urban houses. The culmination is the round hall which is open to the mountain panorama. The construction makes use of reinforced concrete and its capacities for large spans. The columns hidden in the separation walls give the interior lightness and width. Large cantilevers provide the monumental appearance of the exterior.

Vertigo Business Tower

181

SW

109 Bulgaria Boulevard
Panidea Projects/
Raimondo Flaccomio
2012

Situated next to the junction of Bulgaria Boulevard and Sofia Ring Road, close to the green slopes of Vitosha Mountain, the Vertigo Business Tower is quickly and directly accessed from the city centre and also near to the wealthy residential areas of Boyana and Dragalevtsi. The building, whose shape resembles a polished diamond, is surrounded by green landscaped areas. Its 18,300 square metres of flexible office and retail space are distributed over 17 storeys and two underground levels. The tower has a contemporary interior design and includes high-end shopping facilities and cafés. The horizontal part of the complex has a green roof, which helps to optimise the heating and cooling of rooms on the second floor. The façade was custom-developed by Alukönigstahl, and the both the types of glass and the coating reduce solar radiation while conserving heat within the building.

Kopitoto Radio and TV Tower

182

SW

Peak Kopitoto, Vitosha Mountain
Luben Popdonev – Genzo, Stefan Tilev
1977

This needle-like peak is a characteristic component of the silhouette of the Vitosha Mountain when seen from central and southern Sofia. It is a tourist destination, offering panoramic views of the city. The erection of the tower sparked discussion over whether its height of 145 metres would destroy the mountain's silhouette. Together with a lower building, the tower forms part of a complex. The plan is based on a hexagon, in order to achieve statical stability for the tower and to accommodate the lower building in the configuration of the mountain rock. The tower's slim silhouette is interrupted by two cantilevered main platforms which add to the expressiveness with their hexagonal form and varying front lengths. The lower building, which contains studios and technical rooms, is inserted into the opposite slope of the terrain from the tower and so remains invisible from the city. This setup underlines the straight and distinctive appearance of the tower. The complex has established a successful dialogue with its natural surroundings.

Boyana Inclined House
14 Botko Voyvoda Street
I/O architects/Georgi Kytov, Vyara Zhelyazkova
2015

183
SW

Situated on a steep and narrow street near Vitosha Mountain, this project is an attempt to reconcile the opposites in the surrounding area. Buildings in this wealthy area of the city, built-up in the past with small houses and villas, are nowadays rapidly changing scale under the pressure of investments in large residential developments. The shape of this project's plan and its position on the plot provide optimum connections to the yard. The small front elevation and the fragmented façade with variable structures optically decrease the scale of the building's volume. The wooden material of the sliding sun-protection panels relates the building to its natural surroundings. The seemingly uniform external structure, which follows the dynamic terrain, creates complex interconnections between the different levels as well as to the environment. A linear staircase pierces the whole structure, thus increasing the ambiguous relation to the slope. The building's common spaces are organised around its edges.

Boyana Church (St Nikola and St Pantaleymon)

184

SW

3 Boyansko Ezero Street

Restoration: Vassil Kitov.

Wall paintings: Lozinka Koynova and team, 2000; Grigori Grigorov, Vladimir Tsvetkov, 2008

10th–12th, 14th, 16th–17th, and 19th centuries

The church had three construction periods. The oldest structure was built at the turn of the 10th to the 11th century as a single cross-dome space with an apse. It shows typological similarities with the Church of the Holy Saviour in Chora, Istanbul, from the 4th century. The two-storey addition called the Church of Kaloyan was built in 1259. It was named after the ruler of the province of Sredets (medieval Sofia) and church's founder, Sevastocrator Kaloyan, nephew of the Serbian king Stefan Uroš I. The St Nikola narthex on the ground level is thought to have initially been a crypt. The St Pantaleymon cross-dome chapel was located above it. The anteroom on the west side was added in the 19th century. The outer shape of the church clearly expresses the configuration of the internal space and is enriched with vaulted decorative niches. The first church was constructed entirely in brick. The two-step arches end with a so-called 'wolf's tooth' brick bond. The ground level of the Church of Kaloyan is of mixed brick and white stone bond. The chapel on the upper level is of *Opus mixtum* masonry. The arches of the niches are decorated with cup-formed round and square ceramics. The plastering of the dome-cylinder and a reconstruction of the dome of the Church of Kaloyan seem to date from the same period. The high quality of the internationally acclaimed wall paintings in the church is the reason it is

listed as a World Cultural Heritage Site. The original paintings give an overview of the Bulgaria's fine and decorative arts from various periods: 11th–12th centuries, 14th century, and 16th–17th centuries, as well as 1882. The most important paintings are doubtlessly the 89 scenes in the Church of Kaloyan dated from 1259. They are the work of the chief master Vassiliy from the village of Subonosha, next to Serres (now Neo Souli, Greece), the master Dimitriy, and an unknown author. The frescos are considered direct precursors to the Byzantine Palaeologan Renaissance in 1261. The setting of the park around the church was initiated in the beginning of the 20th century by King Ferdinand I, who imported various species of rare plants for it. Ferdinand's second wife, Queen Eleonora, was buried south of the Church of Kaloyan in 1917. A monument to Boyana's war victims stands in the small area in front of the entrance to the church court. Boyana Church has been a branch of the Bulgarian National History Museum since 2003.

Student apartments ↑
5 Kliment Okhridski Boulevard
Amfion Studio
2018

185
SS

Boyana Church reception building and museum ↓
130–132 Brezovitsa Street
Penio Stolarov
1985

186
SW

This building, created from 2016 to 2018, is a free-standing private development situated above the main collector of a thermal power plant. The location necessitated a complex construction solution involving building over a ten-metre-long service tunnel, to height that ensures the passage of a servicing truck, using one-metre-thick reinforced concrete beams and columns. This solution largely determined the architecture. Initially, the building was designed as a student dormitory. The key location and attractive architecture provoked interest and the original project was redeveloped into an apartment building during the construction process. To make this possible, rooms were joined, the laundry and common rooms in the basement were transformed into storage areas, and the number of parking spaces was increased. Despite the complete change of programme, the façade retained the original design and its contrasting white and dark-grey tones.

The design for a reception building with museum for Boyana Church was initiated at the beginning of the 1980s, shortly after the church had been listed by UNESCO as a World Cultural Heritage Site (see 184). The project was carried out from 1983 to 1985. The building was completed as a postmodern interpretation of a basilica typology, referring to the neighbouring Orthodox church in particular. The reception building is a symmetrical structure with a central axis,

a vaulted central hall, and two adjacent volumes. It has two completely different façades. The northern one, which faces the city of Sofia, is divided into three distinct parts and has a fully glazed central entrance area, while the southern façade looks onto Boyana Church and is much more humble in appearance. The red-brick cladding echoes the original brickwork of the church. The building mixes light and dark, ups and downs, and entrance and exit, and culminates in the appearance of the main character in this theatrical architectural game: Boyana Church itself. In 2015 the building was converted into a kindergarten according to a project by the building's original architect, Penio Stolarov.

Paradise Center shopping and entertainment complex

187

S

Cherni Vrah Boulevard/
Henrik Ibsen Street/
Todor Kableshkov Boulevard
RTKL Associates
2016

The Paradise Center is Bulgaria's first lifestyle mall: a complex that combines retail and entertainment spaces. The gross floor area of the shopping centre the amounts to more than 208,000 square metres and the gross leasable area is more than 80,000 square metres. The effect of the interior design is emphasised by decorative motifs that create the sense of outdoor streets set within a park environment. Four interior areas are differentiated in the mall – The Garden, The Canyon, The Terrace, and The Boulevard – each of which stands out with its own concept and design. The sense of luxury is achieved through large volumes and lavish inside spaces, and with high-quality materials and technical facilities.

Assumption of Virgin Mary Monastery

188

S

Dragalevski Road
Church of the Holy Mother of God: 14th and 15th centuries
St Mina Church: 1818
Residence of the Holy Synod:
First restoration, reconstruction, and outbuilding: Alexander Rashenov.
Residence: Panteley Tsvetkov.
Second restoration: Vassil Kitov.
Restoration of wall paintings and icons: Lozinka Koynova, Liubomir Delchev, Valentin Mitkov, Nikolina Yordanova, Yordan Yordanov, Iliana Panova;
1932 (1st restoration and residence),
1992 (2nd restoration),
2016 (icon and painting restoration)

The monastery was founded in the 14th century, but it burned down during the Ottoman invasion in 1382 and was abandoned. The Church of the Holy Mother of God was rebuilt in 1476 with the support of the local ruler Radoslav Mavar. It is a small single-nave church with a dome and a semi-circular apse. The St Mina Church was added to the northern wall in 1818. It was rebuilt and extended with a gallery on the west and north sides in 1932. Both churches were raised and united under a single roof. The eastern elevation was reshaped with a mixed bond of crushed stones and bricks in combination with brick rows. The gallery and the superstructure were shaped in the spirit of the modernist interpretations of National Romanticism from the beginning of the 20th century. The development of the monastery continued throughout the 16th and 17th centuries. The old buildings were refurbished around 1868, and a new two-storey block was added. The complex was once again reconstructed in 1932 by replacing the old buildings with new ones. The Residence of the Holy Synod was built the same year, again in the spirit of modernist National Romanticism. The newest wing of the

monastery was built in the 1980s under the postmodern logic of interventions in a historic context. Three strata of paintings are visible on the church walls: from 1476, and the 16th and 17th centuries. Radoslav Mavar and the pilgrims Kalist and Kraislav are noted as the donators of the wall paintings. Some elements and icons from the iconostasis from 1792–1795 have been restored. After its rebuilding in the 15th century, the monastery was established as a centre for literature and education, with a scriptorium and a school. A great number of gospels, psalter, and other valuable texts were transcribed there, including the Gospel of Dragalevtsi from 1534, today kept in the National Church Museum of History and Archaeology of the Holy Synod, and the Memorial Register of Boyana, written between 1562 and 1612, where the Bulgarian monarchs, patriarchs, donators, and local rulers are listed.

Western Zone

Maps WW, W

The western territories of Sofia lie between the boulevards Slivnitsa and Tsar Boris III. Two decisive urban operations, which started in the middle of the 1950s, were both the initial steps and the motivation to begin the process of urban regeneration and the replacement of the inefficiently-built urban peripheries in poor condition with new housing developments: West Park and the housing estate of the same name. The Lyulin housing estate, the largest in the country, was built in the 1970s to the north-west of the park. The reconstruction of the central territories was implemented in the 1980s. In the 1990s Todor Alexandrov Boulevard, previously a cut-through, became the new western radial axis of the city and opened up new possibilities for the extension of the growing city centre. For a period of about 35 years the western area changed from a territory of lower social and economic status to an integral part of the contemporary Bulgarian capital.

Residential development in Zone B-5

189

W

Aleksandar Stamboliyski Boulevard/Gen. Skobelev Boulevard/Dobrodjanski Krai Street/Kamen Andreev Street Vazrajdane Park:
Veliana Naidenova, Maria Grozeva, Petar Terziev, Angel Yanev
1980

This residential complex was regulated by Sofia's urban development plan from 1972. It was an attempt to completely reconstruct a greater urban territory in Sofia, consisting of several urban blocks. As the area was a part of the city centre, the expected result of the intervention was to be socially beneficial with a great number of new flats. The aim of the urban renewal was to install particular facilities in the area: shops, a school, a kindergarten, social clubs and sports facilities, green areas, and underground parking, as well as a total of 4,987 apartment units on an area of 41.4 hectares. The total floor space is 105,223 square metres and the estimated number of inhabitants about 174,500. The apartments show great diversity in plan and typology: from small lofts and studios to 3–4-bedroom apartments and maisonettes. The height of the blocks varies from 5–6 up to 19–22 floors. The density

of the housing area is 985 inhabitants per hectare, while the density in the entire territory is 422 inhabitants per hectare. Thus, the dwelling space per person is over 25 square metres of floor space and 9.3 square metres of open space, including 5.4 square metres of greenery. The total number of underground parking spaces is 3,430. Before the reconstruction of the territory, its urban block structure was typical for the historic parts of the city: the blocks were set along the streets and were on average 40–45 metres wide. The percentage of street space was relatively high, but the housing stock and infrastructure were run-down and insufficient. The rectangular urban structure was preserved in the course of the reconstruction, but the blocks were joined, in order to offer larger inner courts with underground garages. The master plan respected some existing panel buildings from the 1970s and its aim was to create a dynamic silhouette for the new Zone. Most of the green spaces face the newly constructed Vazrajdane park. Brand characteristics of the architecture are the protruding cantilevers on the upper floors and the exposed reinforced concrete. An industrialised building technique with large-sized concrete formwork was used. The brown clinker brick on the façades provides balance to the otherwise grey structures.

Bulgarian headquarters of International Asset Bank

190

W

81–85 Todor Aleksandrov Boulevard
Zheko Tilev
2003

This building on Todor Aleksandrov Boulevard houses the Bulgarian headquarters and central branch of the International Asset Bank (IAB), as well as a separate section for offices. The architecture is one example of belated postmodernism in Bulgaria: 'high-tech' aesthetics are presented through the sculptural combination of the curvilinear curtain-wall and the rectangular protrusions. The architect, Zheko Tilev, was also responsible for the interior design of the main bank floor and all bank offices. The interior of the building features an interior void that organises the entrances to all main offices and is an integral part of the main banking floor. The building is unique for its construction technology and technical equipment. It is constructed with beamless concrete slabs in combination with spatial steel frames. The building features a light, structural-glass shell and achieves full climate control through a highly efficient and low-energy Variable Refrigerant Volume (VRV) system. It was the first building in the country to have a complex building management system and a licensed heliport.

Lyulin apartment block
Lyulin 6, Bl 647;
647 Dr Peter Dertliev Boulevard
I/O architects/Georgi Kytov, Vyara Zhelyazkova
2009

191
WW

A quarter of a century after the huge Lyulin residential complex was built, the need for new affordable dwellings in the same area arose – as did the need for a new vision. This building embodies the characteristics of two periods and stands on the boundary between nature and the city. It completes Lyulin, gives it a new face, and looks towards Vitosha Mountain. The plan outline visualises the limitations of the planning regulations and maximises the building area, but at the same time gains dynamics from the shape of the plot. The curves of the blind surface complement the geometric ambiguity of the plan. The perforated elevations increase the streamlined appearance of the building. The structure corresponds to the movement along the ring road in front of it. The mass and scale of the building match those of the existing apartment blocks around it. The semi-underground entrance and car park ensure privacy and security.

Northern Zone

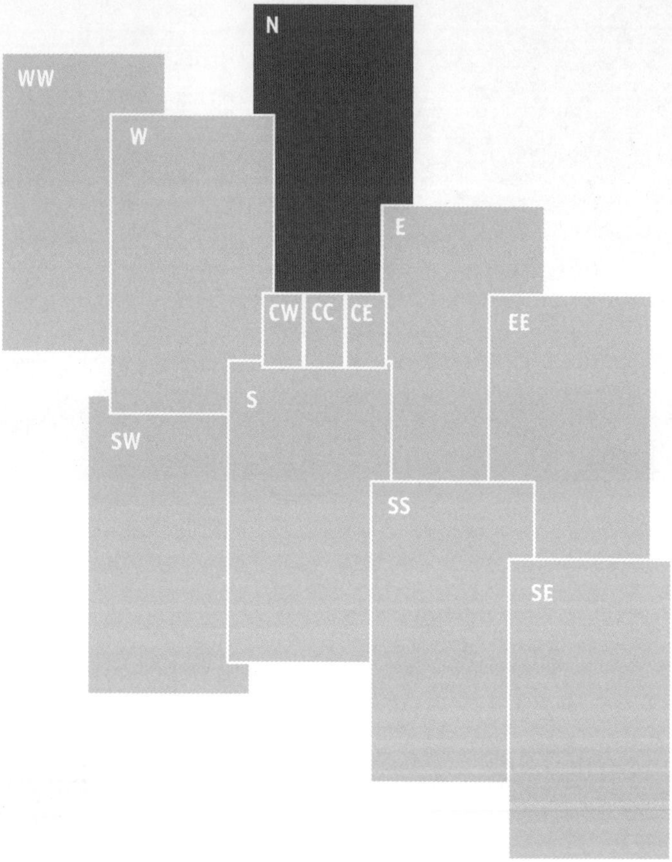

Map N

The northern area of Sofia is associated with the location of the city's Central Railway Station. The first international train from London to Istanbul passed through the newly built station on 12 August 1888. After that, the Orient Express stopped there twice a week. The station introduced the capital city to the Industrial Age and motivated the rearrangement of the public transportation system from horse-drawn buggies to modern electric tramways. The station was a decisive factor for the urbanisation of the area along Knyaginya Maria Luiza Boulevard, which became the basic representative axis of the city. The secondary effect was the incorporation of the Vladaya River into the city's composition as a space for communication and recreation. Combined with the Perlovska River, it created the city's main ring-road around 1900. In the 1940s the river banks were constructed with stone walls and rich vegetation. The 'green necklace' of this infrastructural facility is now a symbol of the city and is partly used as a recreation space. From the beginning of its urbanisation until the present day, the northern area has been an important and sustainable part of both Sofia and Bulgaria's infrastructure. The Central Railway Station was completely rebuilt in 1974. In the 1990s the Central Bus Station was constructed next to it. In addition to the bus and tram systems, the metro links the city to the airport and further afield.

View northwards towards Sofia's industrial zone,
with the cooling towers of the capital's thermo-electric plant

ТЕЦ
СОФИЯ
RUSH

Botev offices and commercial centre

192

N

Hristo Botev Boulevard/Saints Cyril and Methodius Street
Projects GS/Georgi Stanishev
2012

The edifice is situated in the north-western part of Sofia city centre, an area with districts that were predominantly built in the 19th century and a location with a tendency towards reassessment and gentrification. It consists of five office floors on top of three levels of retail space, including one on an underground level. The corner position and the cubic shape of the building allowed for different vertical articulations of its façades. The one facing the narrow street is squeezed in and thus a vertical fold was introduced in order to reduce the perceived scale of the building. The other façade, which faces the boulevard, is a flat surface that further demonstrates the effect of the scale. The window arrangement on this ventilated façade resembles a brick wall. The same simple ornamentation covers both façade surfaces, following the modulations of their shapes: a two-dimensional pattern is mapped onto a three-dimensional volume, creating a peculiar effect. The office on the roof is modelled as a separate self-contained building: an angular penthouse installed on top of the main cube of the edifice, which turns the main block into a sort of pedestal. The gross floor area of the whole complex is 4,800 square metres.

Church of Saints Cyril and Methodius

193

N

47 George Washington Street/Stefan Stambolov Boulevard

Alexi Nachev. Builder: Anton Trifonov. Iconostasis and wood carvings: Gencho Marangozov. Icons: Ivan Dimitrov, Stefan Ivanov, Gospodin Zhelyazkov, Stefan Badjov, Apostol Hristov

1898

This church is part of the ensemble of the Central Market and is located on a fenced plot. It is a three-nave building with a central dome and arched side columns, based on four double columns. In terms of its elevations, the structure is an example of reduced Byzantine architecture, with baroque domes and Lombard bands of arches. This mix of historical styles illustrates the tendencies within Bulgarian National Romantic architecture at the turn of the century. This mixture is also reflected in the interior decoration, which reveals the local arts and crafts of the time. With its Byzantine-Venetian features, the iconostasis evokes interest. The icons were made by the first generation of academically educated Bulgarian artists. Frescoes cover only the central dome.

Locomotive Power Depot, Sofia Central Station

194

N

1–3 Zavodska Street
ca. 1908

The railway depot at Sofia Central Station was built in the early 20th century. It has been reconstructed many times since and nowadays still shelters locomotives. One remarkable element of the depot is the octagonal tower at 3 Zavodska Street, which is the result of several reconstructions. Three to four stages can be easily differentiated. The primary building from the first decade of the 20th century, with its characteristic glazing at the entrance, is clearly readable. There is the one-storey extension – probably from the interwar period. Later alterations took place after the Second World War, when a total of four new levels were constructed in two stages. The windows and details are clearly visible from the outside, as is the load-bearing structure which optically unifies the building. The cantilevers – single on the wall and double at the corners – and powerful columns give a distinctive image to the structure, which strangely resembles a very small-scale paraphrase of the well-known Velasca Tower in Turin, by BBPR studio.

House of the Railway Workers 195

N

106 Maria Luiza Boulevard
Atanas Delibashev,
Ivan Boyadzhiev
1937

The building was planned as a multi-use development, comprising a theatre, a cinema hall, a hotel, meeting rooms, a bar, a restaurant, shops, and offices. Today it functions as a social and cultural centre for employees of the transportation system and as the Seat of the Union of the Transportation Workers Syndicate. In the 1930s critics assessed the building as a 'monument which embodies the cultural development of the epoch'. The architecture seems to have been influenced by the convex and concave elements in Erich Mendelsohn's architecture, especially those seen in the Schocken Department Store in Stuttgart completed in 1926. Atanas Delibashev, who lived in Germany in the 1920s, and finished his architecture studies in Munich in 1928, very likely encountered Mendelsohn's work. The similarity provides the occasion to quote Bruno Zevi's statement on Mendelsohn's department store: 'Many critics have spoken of the musical quality of this building, of the play between inflection and counterpoint.' In this building, the rhythm of the wall articulation becomes lighter as one moves from the bottom to the top. Designed by Delibashev and Ivan Boyadzhiev, it is one of the few examples of expressive modernism in Bulgaria, a style that had a delayed arrival in the context of the European architectural dynamics of the interwar period. The architects used curvilinear glass sheets for the horizontally-striped glass tower, a cylinder that was completely detached from the main structure of the building. Unfortunately, though, the concave-curved glazing was replaced with segments of PVC windows in 2014.

Central Cemetery Park 196 N

11 Kamenodelska Street
1893
Military charnel house:
Petko Tsvyatkov, Alexander Zankov. Reconstruction: Georgi Radoslavov, Boyko Dzhorgov
1930s, 1975 (reconstruction)
Mourning hall and crematorium:
A. Perfanov; 1984
Alley of the Creators, rotunda, urn building:
Zdravets Haitov; 2015

The first burial grounds found in Sofia date back to Antiquity and the Middle Ages, when several necropolises were placed in the city's core territory and on its periphery. The Central Cemetery was the first modern one and is the largest in the city. The terrain for the cemetery was commissioned by the municipal authorities in 1888 and planned in 1893 by unknown architects. The most important reconstruction was carried out in the 1980s, according to the State's decision for the conversion of the cemetery into a memorial park. The total area of the park is 81 hectares. Its composition is based on an orthogonal grid of alleys oriented north–south and east–west.

The main entrance is from the south and is marked with a monumental triple portal with wrought iron gates. The portal was erected during the interwar period and restored according to the original plans in the 1980s. An Orthodox church is situated on the junction between the two wide, green main cross-axes. The contemporary shape of the church was finished in 1967. It was designed by the architect Peter Yoakimov. Two complexes can be distinguished within the cemetery park: the first is the mourning hall with the crematorium connected to it, and the second is the military charnel house built in the 1930s with simplified neo-classical architecture. The family graves of important Bulgarian politicians and public figures are prominently placed in close proximity to the church and along the main alleys. Some of the graves are the work of well-known Bulgarian architects; these include Nikola Lazarov, Ivan Vasilyov, Dimitar Tsolov, and Stancho Belkovski. The greater part of the park is occupied by the Orthodox Christian cemetery. The park contains separate sections for military graves as well as for Muslims, Jews, and followers of the Armenian Apostolic Church.

Central Railway Station
102 Maria Luiza Boulevard
Hans Gerike, Milko Bichev.
Structural engineer:
Svetozar Brankov
1974

197
N

The construction of the station building followed an international architectural competition, which was organised in 1962 and won by an East German team led by Hans Gerike. Because the calculated construction costs exceeded the limit, an adjusted project was planned in 1963 by Milko Bichev and Transproject. The completed building, realised from 1963 to 1974, followed this second project yet kept some key characteristics of the first: a low and wide horizontal body with an airy open space offering a vista of Vitosha Mountain. The functional spaces in and around the

building consist of a plaza, a big reception hall, and an underground system of subways and shops leading to the train tracks. The station introduces a circulation scheme on two levels: a main level for international connections, accessed directly from the plaza, and an underground level for domestic connections, accessible from the open rotunda in the underground passages. The reinforced concrete construction is deliberately exposed at the fronts of the building, facing the plaza and the platforms. Its 18 X-shaped columns of raw concrete support the space-frame roof construction with its 11-metre cantilever.

Lions' Bridge

198

N

Maria Luiza Boulevard/
Slivnitsa Boulevard
Adolf Václav Kolář, Václav Prošek
Metal sculptures: R. P. Waagner
1889, 1891 (sculptures)

A bridge over the Vladayska River existed at this location as early as the 3rd–4th century. The facility was part of the Roman Via Militaris (Via Diagonalis, Via Singidunum) which connected Singidunum (now Belgrade) with Constantinople (now Istanbul). The construction of a new bridge during Ottoman rule was initiated by Halil Sali Effendi. The bridge (Sandikli Kupru) was decorated with red and yellow stripes and was therefore popularly known as the 'Colourful Bridge'. On both sides of the bridge passers-by could see inscriptions which no longer exist: 'I sold in time and created a bridge' and 'Where there is no bridge – build one. Where there is no spring – build one.' The contemporary Lions' Bridge, which replaced the Colourful Bridge, is part of a larger memorial to four national revolutionists who were hanged there during the Ottoman period. Their tragic death was described by Dick de Lonley, a correspondent for the newspapers *Le Monde illustré* and *La Moniteur universel*. The figures of the four lions symbolise the four victims. The lions and the candelabra were designed and produced by the Viennese company Rudolph Philip Waagner in 1891. The bridge was the main entrance to the city until the end of the 1920s, and connected the Central Railway Station with the political and administrative city centre. The Lions' Bridge was recently restored in the course of a reconstruction of the nearby square for a new traffic solution and the construction of the metro station.

Sofia Slaughterhouse (former Rodopa Meat Processing Factory)

199

N

1 Malashevska Street
Boris Bobchev, Petar Markovski, Walter Sanzin
1932

Sofia Slaughterhouse was built after a competition in 1928. It was designed to meet the needs of the entire population of the city and was the most up-to-date type of abattoir at the time. The complex is situated on a triangular plot, and its layout is a combination of arched longitudinal and fan-shaped transversal buildings. This arrangement not only met the technological requirements but also permitted the development of the architectural and aesthetic concept. The curvilinear outlines of the plan created a dynamic interior space with a modern appearance. The pointed-arch motif is implemented in different scales and positions, giving the complex a sense of unity. The imposing size of the entrance façade, along with the tower in the background, creates associations with the monumentality of a medieval fortress.

St George the Victorious Monastery

200

N

Kremikovtsi

Restoration: Stoyan Yanev

Wall paintings: Lyuba Krasovska, Zamfir Petrov

14th century, 1493, 1979 (restoration), 2000 (wall paintings)

The monastery was founded in the middle of the 14th century. It was destroyed by the Ottomans in 1382 and rebuilt by the local landlord Radivoy in 1493, in memory of his deceased children Teodor and Dragana. In the same period the old St George Church was reconstructed and painted. It is a small, vaulted space with two anterooms and a semi-circular apse. The church was renewed in 1611. A second anteroom was added on the eastern side at the beginning of the 20th century, preserving the wall paintings from the 17th century. The modest architecture creates a chamber effect, whereas the varied pointillist surface of the nuke-masonry, crowned with a cornice in 'wolf's tooth' brick bond, carries an expressive image. The wall paintings in the naos date from the 15th century. Scenes from the life of St George were painted on the eastern side. Portraits of Radivoy and his family, Kalevit the Bishop of Sofia, and the church's patron were painted on the northern side. The rest of the frescos are from the 17th century. The monastery was a great educational and spiritual centre, where the Gospel of Kremikovtsi was produced in 1497. The new church, the Intercession of the Mother of God, was built in 1907. It is a central cross-dome building with an anteroom and a bell tower. The iconostasis is made by the wood-carver family Filipov from the village of Ossoy, near Debar. The monastery keeps relics from St George of Sofia the New, a martyr burned by the Ottomans in 1515 because of his Christian religion.

View along Knyaginya Maria Luiza Boulevard towards the city centre and Vitosha Mountain

Apartment building, 135 Rakovski St, unknown architect, 1930s

Lozenets apartment building, 28 Dimitar Hadzhikotsev St, architect: AEDES Studio, 2010

National Health Institute, 26 Yanko Sakuzov Blvd, architects: Todor Zlatev and Dimitar Koev, 1932

Apartment building, Trapezitsa/George Washington St, architect: Maria Sapareva, 1935

Private residence, door, architect: AEDES Studio, 2006

The collection of photos for 'Sofia in Detail' was provided for publication by:
- Bulgarian Modernist Architecture
- AEDES Studio
- I/O architects
- Projects GS Studio

Index of Objects

Archaeological remains and architectural objects from Antiquity, the Middle Ages, and the Ottoman Period:

Objects from the post-Liberation period, 1878–1918, which present the influences of European neo-historic styles, eclecticism, art nouveau, and Bulgarian National Romanticism:

Objects from the interwar period 1918–1944, which present the influences of modernist tendencies and the revival of classicism:

Objects in the classicist style from the postwar Stalinist era:

Objects in the modernist style from the socialist peiod:

Objects from the post-socialist period:

Index of Persons

Architects, artists, and other experts related to the objects from Antiquity, the Middle Ages, and the Ottoman period:

Architects, artists, and other experts related to the objects from the post-Liberation period, 1878–1918:

Architects, artists, and other experts related to the objects from the interwar period, 1918–1944:

Architects, artists and other experts related to the classicist style from the postwar Stalinist era:

Architects, artists, and other experts related to modernism during the socialist period:

Architects of the objects of the post-socialist period:

Bibliography

Selected Sources in Cyrillic Script

Аврамов, И.: Съвременно градоустройство в България, Техника София 1987

Архитектурата в България 1878-1944. БАН-ИТИГА София 1978

Белковски, Ст.: Архитектурна дейност 1922-1942. Жилища, обществени сгради, селища.

Булев, Т.: Следвоенното развитие на българската архитектура 1944-2006. Архитектура София 5 2007, 90-91

Василиев, А.: Резбарски род на Филиповци от с. Осой, Македонска мисъл 1 1946

Василиев, А.: Български възрожденски майстори: живописци, резбари, строители. Наука и изкуство 1965

Ганевъ, Н.: Паметницить на столица София, София 1939

Ганчев Хр.: Композиция и оптически мащаб на някои архитектурни пространства в централната градска част на София, Сб. "Проучвания и консервация на паметниците на културата в България",том II, Техника София 1983, 77-82

Ганчев, Хр.: София - улици и площади. Планово и обемно-пространствено проучване, КК-НИПК, София 1983

Ганчев Хр.: Историко-градоустройствени проучвания на историческото ядро на град София, Опазване на културрното наследство в България, НИПК и ЦПИП-КК, София 1984, 55-66

Ганчев, Хр.: "Проучвания и проект за фасадна реставрация на църквата "Св.София"/1980-1981 г. /, Сб. "Проучвания и консервация на паметниците на културата в България, том III, НИПК и ЦПИП-КК, София 1984, 132-140

Ганчев, Хр./Г. Дойчинов: Европейски влияния върху българската архитектура: 1878-1919, Архитектура, София 3/2000, 60-63, 4/2000, 67-71, 5/2000, 38-41, 6/2000, 46-49

Ганчев, Хр./Дойчинов Гр.: Градоустройството в България 1878–1918, Архитектура 2/2001, 19–23

Ганчев, Х.: Дворцовата архитектура в контекста на архитектурното развитие в началото на XX век в България, Научна конференция "Епохата на Цар Фердинанд I" – I част, Евксиноград 2008, ЖЛМ 2008, 84-101

Ганчев, Хр.: Дворцовата архитектура на Третото българско царство, Научна конференция "Епохата на Цар Фердинанд I" - II част, София 2008, ЖЛМ 2009, 17-25

Ганчев Хр.: Историческа справка и градоустройствен модел на гр.София, Наръчник на международният симпозиум на ИКОМОС и ИККРОМ "Научни методи за опазване на паметта на един град - проблеми на формирането", НИПК София 1990, 8-23

Ганчев, Х./Г. Дойчинов/И. Стоянова: България 1900. Европейски влияния в българското градоустройство, архитектура, паркове и градини 1878-1918, АРХ&АРТ София 2002

Ганчев, Хр.: Историко-археологически резерват Сердика – Средец, сборник Културно-исторически резервати в България, НИПК София 2003, 112-114

Генчев, Хр.: София мислена в пространството, АрхЛИБРИ София 2009

Генчев, Хр: Българското Възраждане, София 1988

Дойчинов, Гр./Хр. Ганчев: Формирането на старите градски части на София и подходът към тях, НИПК София 1989
Желева, Д./Ю. Фърков: История на Българското градоустройство XIX-XX век. Диахронни анализи, БАН-ЦА, София 2009
Киселков, В. С. Софийската духовна семинария. Сердика 10/1938
Койчев, П.: Съдебната палата в София, БАН - ИГА, София 1956
Лабов, Г.: Архитектурата на София. Техника София 1979
Миков, Л.: Османска архитектура и изкуство в България, том I, Проф. Марин Дринов 2012
Монеджикова, А.: София през вековете. Факел София 1946
Предложение за обявяване на паметници на културата от периода 1878-1944. НИПК София 1977
Протичъ, А.: Архитектоническата форма на софийската църква Св. София, Царска придворна печатница София 1912
Решетникова, О. Н.: Русская церковь в Софии. С. 2010
Сердика, Средец, София, том 3, МИС София 1997
Софийската духовна семинария 1907-1932, Юбилейна книга, София 1932
Станишев, Г. Архитектурата на вечното настояще. Локално и глобално в съвременната българска Архитектура. Списание Архитектура. 2005, № 1-2
Станишев, Г. Интерфейс София или критика на визуалното очарование. – Култура, 2010, № 7, 26 февруари.
Сто години Софийска духовна семинария „Св. Йоан Рилски“, Юбилеен сборник, София 2005
Съвременно българско монументално изкуство 1956-1986, КК, П. Берон София 1986
Ташев, П.: София – архитектурно-градоустройствено развитие. Техника София 1972
Торньов, А., Новопостроеният храм "Св. Мъченица Параскева". Архитект 1930, бр. 3-4
Филов, Б,: Софийската църква Света София, Царска придворна печатница София 1913
Фомина, Л.: Градини и паркове на България. Арх & Арт София 2007
Фомина, Л.: Паркът Врана. Земиздат София 2003
Юбилейна книга на градъ София (1878-1928), Книпеграфъ АД София 1928

Bibliography

Selected Sources in Latin Script

Bohn, T. M., and Calic M.(ed.): *Urbanisierung und Stadtentwicklung in Südosteuropa*, Otto Sagner München, 2010.

Delmard, A.: 'The Park and Grounds of Vrana. One of Residences of His Majesty King Ferdinand of Bulgaria', in *The Journal of the Royal Horticultural Society,* XXXVII, part III, 1912.

Doytchinov, G.: 'Die Verwirklichung des Ringstraßensystems in Sofia', in *Berichte zur Raumforschung und Raumplanung,* 33, 1–2, 1989, pp. 26–34.

Doytchinov, G., and Ganchev, H. : *Österreichische Architekten in Bulgarien 1878-1918,* Böhlau Wien, 2001.

Doytchinov, G.: *Das pluralistische Experiment. Widersprüche und Potentiale der mitteleuropäischen Stadt*, TU Graz, 2002.

Doytchinov, G., Djukic, A., and Jonita, C.: *Planning Capital Cities: Belgrade, Bucharest, Sofia*, TU Graz, 2015.

Doytchinov, G., and Ganchev, Ch.: 'Arhitektur im Diskontinum', in *Architektur & BauForum,* 4, 2000.

Gantchev, Ch.: Art Nouveau Architecture in Bulgaria: Development and National Examples, Art Nouveau/Jugendstil Architecture in Europe, Deutsche UNESCO-Kommission, Bonn 1988, pp. 26–36.

Gantchev, Ch.: List of the preserved buildings with stylistic features of art nouveau architecture in Sofia city centre, Deutsche UNESCO-Kommission Newsletter, 2, 1988, pp. 21–43.

Gantchev, Ch., Kantardjieva A., and Kitov, V.: Two examples of the approach to the architecture of Romanticism in Bulgaria, Deutsche UNESCO-Kommission Newsletter, 2, 1988, pp. 44–50.

Gantchev, Ch.: The Sofia National Museum 'Man and Earth' and the Approach to Early 20th Century Traditional Buildings, Deutsche UNESCO-Kommission Newsletter, 3, 1990, pp. 49–52.

Gantchev, Ch.: Restoration of the Vrana Palace complex, art nouveau/Jugendstil architecture, Finnish National Commission for UNESCO, Helsinki 1991, pp. 124–131.

Ganchev, Ch.: Bulgarian Architecture in the 1920s and 30s, DOCOMOMO, Eindhoven University of Technology, 1991, pp. 141–144.

Ganchev, H.: Historical and Archaeological Reserve Serdica: Sredets Cultural and Historical Reserves in Bulgaria, Sofia 2003, pp. 112–114.

Stanishev, G.: 'Der Discrete Charme der Peripherie', in *Bulgarien: architektonische Fragmente*, Stiller, Adolf (ed.), Anton Pustet, Wien, 2007.

Stanishev, G. (Sr) and Stanishev, Georgi (Jr): 'Notes on Centres and Peripheries in Eastern Bloc Architectures', pp. 45–66 in *Re-Framing Identities. Re-building Europe, 1950-1990,* Moravánszky, Ákos, and Lange, Torsten (eds), De Gruyter Akademie Forschung, Birkhäuser, 2017.

Credits

Authors and Contributors

Boulev, Todor: 009, 018, 033, 049, 056, 092, 097, 115, 117, 122, 123, 124, 125, 126, 127, 137, 140, 154, 155, 160 161, 167, 168, 169, 172, 180, 182, 188, 196, 197.
Boyadzhiev, Konstantin: 019, 021, 064, 094, 109, 110.
Bratkova, Rossitsa: 100, 131, 162, 166, 173, 179.
Doytchinov, Grigor: 006, 011, 012, 013, 023, 029, 030, 031, 032, 038, 039, 040, 041, 042, 043, 047, 050, 053, 055, 057, 059, 066, 067, 071, 076, 077, 083, 087, 095, 096, 099, 102, 103, 105, 106, 119, 142, 143, 148, 152, 158, 193.
Ganchev, Hristo: chapter introductions, 001, 002, 003, 004, 005, 007, 008, 010, 014, 015, 016, 017, 024, 025, 026, 034, 044, 045, 048, 051, 054, 058, 060, 061, 062, 063, 068, 069, 070, 072, 073, 074, 075, 078, 079, 080, 081, 084, 086, 088, 089, 089, 093, 098, 104, 107, 108, 118, 121, 139, 156, 159, 164, 184, 188, 194, 198, 200.
Kanalieva, Teodora: 027, 028, 037, 141, 144, 145, 146, 149, 150, 151, 194, 199.
Makarinov, Vassil, and Karakolev, Theodor: 22, 35, 46, 82, 91, 114, 116, 147.
Stanishev, Georgi: 'The Maps: Connecting History and Geography', 018, 020, 033, 113, 170, 178, 192.
Vassileva, Aneta: 111, 112, 122.

Texts for the works built in the period 1990–2018 were prepared by the authors of the buildings with some adjustments by the editor. These are: 036, 052, 092, 100, 101, 120, 128, 129, 130, 131, 132, 133, 134, 135, 136, 137, 138, 162, 163, 165, 166, 171, 173, 174, 175, 176, 177, 179, 181, 183, 187, 190, 191.

Credits

Images

The credits are according to page number. If the position of the image is not specified, then all the images on the page are by that author.

Key
t = top, b = bottom, l = left,
r = right, m = middle

+Architectura: 199b.
A&A Architects: 201, 204–205, 244.
AEDES Studio: 7, 166, 231, 243, 249.
Ahsmann, Mark [CC BY-SA 4.0]/ Wikimedia Commons: 236b, 237t, 240.
Apostoloff [CC BY-SA 3.0]/Wikimedia Commons: 67t, 167b.
Apostoloff [GPL (http://www.gnu.org/licenses/gpl.html)]/Wikimedia Commons: 250b.
Architectonika Studio: 241.
Anastas Tarpanov [CC BY-SA 2.0]/ Wikimedia Commons: 143b.
Atelier Serafimov Architects: 200.
Bulgarian Modernist Architecture: 78, 79t, 84bl, 84br, 94t, 100, 101t, 111b, 146, 157b, 182tl, 182tr, 116t, 187, 214, 216t, 217t, 220b, 221, 273, 274t, 278.
City Media Group: 18, 35, 158, 196, 276.
Creative-Family/iStock: 212.
Deensel [CC BY 2.0]/Wikimedia Commons: 62–63, 70–71, 90–91, 98–99, 104–105, 112–113, 116–117, 126–127, 132–133, 140–141, 144–145, 190–191, 226–227, 225b, 268–269, 280–281.
Destructive Creation: 165t.
Didi Lavchieva/iStock: 64t.
Doytchinov, Grigor: 229.
Doytchinov, Grigor/Petev, Georgi: 12.
Elite Architecture Studio: 245.
Eminov, Tyuncher: 16–17.
Emil Ivanov/iStock: 76.
Font83/iStock: 55t.
Fordewind Architecture: 207.
Ganchev, Hristo: 41b, 43bl, 43br; private archive: 59b, 131b, 209b.
Guentchev, Christo: 69b.
Gyupchanova, Maria: 38–39t, 39m, 41t, 40b, 43t, 44, 45t, 48–49t, 50–51, 52bl, 52br, 53, 54, 56, 57, 58b, 60, 61, 64b, 67b, 72, 73t, 74t, 77, 79bl, 82, 83, 87, 88, 89, 93b, 94b, 97, 107b, 118, 119, 122, 124, 125, 128, 131t, 134, 135t, 136, 137, 138, 139b, 142bl, 142br, 147, 151t, 152, 154–155,156, 157, 159b, 160, 161, 164, 168, 169, 170, 171, 176b, 177b, 178, 179, 180, 184b, 185, 193b, 206, 208, 215, 216b, 224, 225b, 232, 238t, 242, 252b, 254, 255t, 258, 259, 262–263, 271, 277, 279, 296.
Hdesislava/iStock: 153t.
Hubertgui/Wikimedia Commons: 153b.
I/O architects: 253, 265.
Courtesy of Ivan Vazov National Theatre: 97b.
Ivo Petrov Architects: 195b.
Kikagogo/iStock: 66b, 121.
LP Group: 85, 197, 223, 235.
Mariusz_prusaczyk/iStock: 4.
Meuser, Philipp: 45br, 49b, 65, 73b, 80, 81, 84t, 86, 106b,108, 109, 110, 111t, 129b, 130, 148, 149, 174–175, 182b, 183b, 184t, 189b, 195t, 198, 199t, 213b, 217b, 219t, 228.
MrPanyGoff [CC BY-SA 3.0 or GFDL]/Wikimedia Commons: 225t.
MYS Architects: 167, 246b, 247b.
Courtesy of the National Museum Complex: 150, 151b.
Nenko Lazarov [CC BY 2.5] NIM/ Wikimedia Commons: 250t.
Nikolai Karaneschev [CC BY 3.0]: 59t.
Ollirg/iStock: 69t.
Panidea Studio: 251.
Plamen Agov [CC BY-SA 3.0 or GFDL] studiolemontree.com/Wikimedia Commons: 93t, 237b, 142t, 165b, 189.

ProArch studio: 102, 103, 186, 257.
Pudelek (Marcin Szala) [CC BY-SA 3.0]/ Wikimedia Commons: 92b.
Courtesy of Regional History Museum of Sofia: 8, 9, 10, 11; 42b.
Sjhaytov/iStock: 68, 213t.
Courtesy of Sofiazanas.blogspot.bg: 95bl.
Courtesy of Spas (foursquare.com): 181t.
Courtesy of Stara Sofia: 45bl.
STARH Studio: 246t.
Courtesy of Svetoslav Nikolov, National Opera and Ballet Theatre: 123b.
Courtesy of TIIIM, Wikimapia, from the Ministry of Agriculture, Food and Forestry: 165t.
Tilev Architects: 264.
Tornyov, Peter (private archive): 138.
Vassia Atanassova - Spiritia [GFDL or CC BY-SA 3.0]/Wikimedia Commons: 230b.
Vili45/iStock: 253t.
WhATA: 181t, 188t, 230t.
Stanishev, Georgi: 23–34, 38b, 39b, 52t, 55b, 58t, 76b, 79br, 94b, 95t, 96b, 101b, 106tl, 106tr, 107t, 123t, 135b, 159t, 181b, 192, 193t, 194, 202–203, 218, 219b, 220t, 222br, 223, 229b, 233, 235, 239, 248, 256t, 270, 272, 274b, 275.

The photos for the article 'Sofia in Detail' were provided by Bulgarian Modernist Architecture, Georgi Stanishev, AEDES Studio, I/O Architects, Hristo Ganchev.

Authors

Konstantin Boyadzhiev *(author, editorial board member)* is an architect and professor at the University of Architecture, Civil Engineering and Geodesy (UACEG), Sofia, and an expert in the history and theory of architecture. He was a director of the Centre for Architectural Studies of the Bulgarian Academy of Sciences. He teaches at the New Bulgarian University and is a guest lecturer at the UACEG, the Lyuben Karavelov University of Structural Engineering and Architecture, Sofia, and other universities in Bulgaria and abroad. He has published numerous works on the history of Bulgarian architecture.

Rossitsa Bratkova *(author, text editor)* is a practicing architect with a Master's degree in Architectural Theory and Criticism. She teaches at the UACEG, Sofia, and was a guest lecturer at the ENSAS, Strasbourg, and at MSA, Münster. She has published several works in the field of architecture theory and criticism. She is a co-founder of AEDES Studio, a practice which has won various national and international awards.

Todor Boulev *(author, editorial board member)* is an architect and professor of Urbanism at the Varna Free University 'Chernorizets Hrabar' and guest lecturer at the Lyuben Karavelov University of Structural Engineering and Architecture, and the National Academy of Arts, Sofia. His field of expertise is urban and landscape design in theory and freelance practice, as proved by more than 300 publications.

Bulgarian Modernist Architecture *(authors and illustration providers)* concentrates on the history of interwar Modern Movement architecture in Bulgaria. The group conducts historical research, documentation, and educational activities, and consists of two art historians who have worked together since 2014: **Vassil Makarinov**, a curator at the National Polytechnic Museum, and **Theodor Karakolev**, an art journalist. In 2017 the group has created the travelling exhibition 'Bulgarian Modernist Architecture: Examples from the 1920s, 1930s, and 1940s', which visited a number of Bulgarian cities.

Grigor Doytchinov *(author, editorial board member)* is an architect and professor for Urbanism at the Graz University of Technology. He was a member of the jury for the Europa Nostra/European Union Award for Cultural Heritage and the Expert Commission for the Preservation of Graz Historic Centre. He leads projects for the European Union and the Austrian Ministry of Foreign Affairs, and has numerous publications on the history of urbanism in Central Europe.

Hristo Ganchev *(author, editorial board member)* is an architect and an expert at the National Institute for Monuments of Culture and the Ministry of Culture. He is a researcher, theoretician, and designer in the fields of conservation and urban preservation. He is a participant in the UNESCO International Joint Cultural Study and Action Project for the Preservation of Art Nouveau/Jugendstil Architectural Heritage; DOCOMOMO, and other organisations. He has over 50 international publications.

Teodora Kanalieva Dimitrova *(author, consultant)* is an architect and assistant professor at the University of Architecture, Civil Engineering and Geodesy (UACEG). Her main field of interest is the history of Bulgarian architecture with a focus on modernist architecture from the period between the two world wars. She also works in the field of history of European architecture from the 15th to the 19th centuries.

Georgi Stanishev *(author, editor, editorial board member)* is an architect and architecture publicist, professor of the Theory and History of Architecture at the University of Architecture, Civil Engineering and Geodesy (UACEG), Sofia, and the International Academy of Architecture, Moscow. Stanishev is Vice President of the Iakov Chernikhov International Foundation, Moscow/Sofia. He has published several monographs and numerous articles in the international architecture press.

Aneta Vassileva *(author)* is an architectural historian, critic, and publicist, and a member of WhAT Association (WhATA). She teaches at the University of Architecture, Civil Engineering and Geodesy (UACEG) and holds a PhD in Architectural History and Theory, focused on postwar architecture, from the same university. Vassileva contributes to the European Council programme ATRIUM (Architecture of Totalitarian Regimes of the 20th Century in Urban Management) and a member of the A10 New European Architecture Cooperative.

Acknowledgements
This book would not have been completed without the support and assistance of several institutions. Special thanks go to:

- The National Institute of Immovable Cultural Heritage
- The National Historical Museum
- The National Archaeological Institute with Museum – Bulgarian Academy of Sciences
- The Directorate of Religious Affairs at the Council of Ministers
- The Regional History Museum – Sofia
- Prophets of religions temples
- Ivan Vazov National Theatre
- National Opera and Ballet Theatre
- Bulgarian Modernist Architecture blog
- Stara Sofia blog
- Destructive Creation group

The Deutsche Bibliothek lists this publication in the Deutsche Nationalbibliografie; detailed bibliographic data is available online at http://dnb.d-nb.de

ISBN 978-3-86922-657-6

Text editor
Rossitsa Bratkova

Proofreading
Amy Visram

Design
Georgi Stanishev

Final artwork
Masako Tomokiyo

Printing
Tiger Printing (Hong Kong) Co., Ltd
www.tigerprinting.hk

DOM
publishers

Allianz

Staircase in an apartment building at
21 Dyakon Ignatiy St, first half of 1930s

Sofia in Detail

Rossitsa Bratkova

Ludwig Mies van der Rohe: 'God is in the detail.'
English proverb: 'The devil is in the detail.'

Buildings emit messages on three levels with regard to the distance from which we perceive them. The first, and coarsest, is their urban appearance as volumes and silhouettes by which they declare their presence in the city skyline. As we move closer, we pass through the second level, in which a building's scale is revealed by the proportions of the solid walls and the openings in them, but more importantly through the defining of some physicality through the volumes and the building materials. Finally, we come to the third level: direct contact, face to face with the building. For it is only then, at a close distance, that the building reveals its most individual features, its physiognomy. Close proximity to a beautiful building often evokes the desire for a more sensuous type of contact, for the physical touch of its skin. The sight of some lovely polished stone on a façade awakens a deep atavistic instinct that does not allow us to rely upon our eyes and reason alone. Instead, it requires us to explore further – through the touch of our fingertips.

So, while we move from large to small, from the urban scale to the detail, we are in fact moving from an abstract way of perceiving a building as an element of the urban landscape towards recognising it as a tangible presence in that landscape. More precisely, it is in the unobstructed visual relation from the other side of the street that we as observers can notice and treasure in our memory that strange, eclectic, and often disintegrating language of the past spoken by the old buildings of Sofia. Details are the words of architectural language that bring architecture closer to the passer-by and make it much clearer and easy to recognise for the non-specialist. I have always thought that it is the cognoscibility and conspicuousness of early-20th-century architectural details that make buildings of the period so beloved by Sofia's citizens. The details speak directly, almost intimately, and thus make the faces of buildings clearly recognisable and easy to remember. The viewer need not know about the history of architecture or be a connoisseur of the various styles of the past.

Nedkov apartment building, 48 Vitosha Blvd, architects: Radoslav Radoslavov and Konstantin Dzhangozov, 1937–1938

Apartment building, 28 Patriarch Evtimiy Blvd, architect: Vasko Vassilev, 1935

Apartment building, 7 William Gladstone St, unknown architect, early 1930s

Apartment building, 96 Knyaz Boris St, unknown architect, ca. 1940

Apartment building, 28 Vitosha Blvd, architect: Vasko Vassilev, late 1930s

Apartment building, 98 Patriarch Evtimiy Blvd, unknown architect, late 1930s

Workers' Hospital (today Queen Giovanna Hospital), 8 Byalo More St, architect: Georgi Ovcharov, project: 1927, built: 1930–1935

Apartment building, 86 Vitosha Blvd, architect: Kiril Otsetov, early 1940s

Isola apartment building, 24 Evlogi and Christo Georgievi Blvd, unknown architect, 1933

Apartment building, 28 Patriarch Evtimiy Blvd, architect: Vasko Vassilev, 1935

Balabanov's house, 3 Oborishte St, architect: Maria Berova-Haning, 1938

Cooperative apartment building, 27 William Gladstone St, architect: Vasko Vassilev, 1943

National Stdent House, 10 National Assembly Sq, architects: Stancho Belkovski and Ivan Danchov, 1931–1933

Hotel complex and Bulgaria Concert Hall, 4 Tsar Osvoboditel Blvd, architects: Stancho Belkovski and Ivan Danchov, 1934–1937

EMIVAN staircase of single family house, Bankya district, architect: Projects GS, 2009

Sirak Skitnik's house, 28 Borova Gora St, architect: Georgi Ovcharov, 1926

Cooperative apartment building, 27 William Gladstone St, architect: Vasko Vassilev, 1939-43

Private house extension, 19 Oborishte St, architect: I/O architects, 2012

Knyaginya Evdokia Kindergarten, Alexandrovska Hospital, architect: Konstantin Dzhangozov, 1936

Angel Kantardzhiev's house, Tzar Osvoboditel Blvd, architects: Ivan Vasilyov and Dimitar Tsolov, project: 1932

Angel Kantardzhiev's house, Tzar Osvoboditel Blvd, architects: Ivan Vasilyov and Dimitar Tsolov, project: 1932

Cooperative apartment building, 27 William Gladstone St, architect: Vasko Vassilev, 1943

Apartment building stairs, 1 Strumitsa St, unknown architect, late 1930s

Lozenets apartment building, 28 Dimitar Hadzhikotsev St, architect: AEDES Studio, 2010

Apartment building, 45 General Gurko St, architect: Vasko Vassilev, late 1930s

Angel Kantardzhiev's house, Tzar Osvoboditel Blvd, architects: Ivan Vasilyov and Dimitar Tsolov, project: 1932

Apartment building, 27 Moskovska St, architects: Georgi Manafov and St Panchev, mid-1930s

National Health Institute, 26 Yanko Sakazov Blvd, architects: Todor Zlatev and Dimitar Koev, 1932

Apartment building, 37 Moskovska St, architect: Viktoria Angelova-Vinarova, 1937

Ivan Marinov's apartment building, 5 Patriarch Evtimiy Blvd, unknown architect, 1937

7th primary school 'St. Sedmochislenitsi', 28 Tsar Shishman St, architects: Maria Sapareva and Mara Zakharieva, 1933–1935

Apartment building, 9 Oborishte St, architect: Angel Momov, 1930s

Single family house, 15 Nikolay Rakitin St, unknown architect, 1930s

St Paraskeva Church, 58 Georgi Sava Rakovski St, architect: Anton Torniov, 1930; Iconostasis: Todor Hristov, Ivan Travnitzki, 1940

Hotel complex and Bulgaria Concert Hall, 4 Tsar Osvoboditel Blvd, architects: Stancho Belkovski and Ivan Danchov, 1934–1937

POPO single family residence, Simeonovo district, architects: Projects GS, 2000

There are consistent lines of referential influences adopted by the city. These have undergone multiple reinterpretations throughout history but can still be traced back to their origin. The Byzantine architectural tradition probably had the strongest impact through powerful examples such as the Hagia Sophia in Constantinople (now Istanbul). Some features of the cathedral (the building initially served as a cathedral and later as a mosque) were imported to Boyana Church (184) during the Middle Ages, and then subsequently adopted by the Ottoman tradition as well in Buyuk Mosque (now the National Archaeological Museum; 026), the 'Roman Wall' (159), and St Sedmochislenitsi Church (054).

In the course of their interpretation, details play the role of meaning-defining features. In the Byzantine tradition, for instance, the dome is set upon pendentives, as is in the St Sofia Church (061), while the Ottoman tradition uses squinches as in the Banya Bashi Mosque (025). In this way, the Seven Saints Church, today an Orthodox place of worship, has preserved memories from its time as a mosque through its squinches – a feature otherwise uncommon in Orthodox architecture – which make the transition between the half-sphere of the dome to the corner columns that form the square of the base.

In the context of the stylistic variety of details from the beginning of the 20th century, there is a certain group that deserves special attention. The authors of these buildings did not merely adopt European trends as the blueprints for their designs, but rather turned their gaze back to the roots of the Bulgarian national architectural tradition. In that synthesis, some highly specific National Romantic façades were created – the Public Mineral Baths (007) and the Theological Faculty of Sofia University (015) being the most prominent of them. Their double rows of red brick and ceramic-tile ornamentation echo similar motifs from the churches in Tarnovo and Nessebar from the time of the Second Bulgarian Empire. Though linked to the past, National Romanticism was a reinterpretation, as is the case with every real renaissance. The lushness and garrulity of the architectural details was, to a large extent, tamed by modernism which gradually appeared from the 1930s onwards. Brought from Western Europe by a generation of architects who received their education there, modernism gave up the detail as an ornament in the way it was commonly known until then. The modernist detail became more sophisticated, more connected to contemporary architectural solutions, to the designing of new forms and not to the repetition of old ones. The new detail followed directly from the essence of the building; it was not added as a separate system of elements. Changes in construction methods also played a large role in that process. Whereas before modernism eclectic details were roughly outlined by the architect and then skilfully handcrafted on-site by artisans practised in the work, this element of craftsmanship slowly began to fade away in modernist buildings. Modernist details are, to a much greater degree, a product of the mind rather than a product of the hand. That is probably one of the reasons why they often remain unappreciated by people who are not interested in architecture. Objects made by a talented human hand receive an intuitive understanding and appreciation, while the fruits of intellectual work require a corresponding effort from the viewer.

The involvement of the observer in the reading of the building, his or her participation in its text as a reader, is now becoming an ever more common feature of contemporary architecture. Details penetrate deeper and deeper into the flesh of a building; they have already become a part of its construction. Today, cleverly thought-out details can be grasped behind straight lines, delicate proportions, a grid of joints. As they remain hidden behind the outer skin of the building, details now create a peculiar enigmatic air which rouses curiosity and questions such as 'How is a big cantilever support?', 'How is the window frame so thin?', and so on.

Architectural details change over the course of time. Ornamentation has disappeared from the places where we were used to see it – around window openings and doorways, at the point of contact between a facade and a roof. Areas of transition – between the different elements of a building, between inside and outside – are intermediate zones that require a special design approach.

Modernist architecture replaced the ornaments with an entirely different type of detail and frequently changed the location of the detail. For instance, decoration around window frames was displaced by an entire window or a horizontal stripe of windows. Continuing that trend, late modernity turned the entirety of a building into one immense detail, deliberately dramatising its silhouette. The architecture of today, released from Adolf Loos's correlation between ornament and crime, has rediscovered the ornament – not as a single image any more but as a motif which covers entire surfaces. Sometimes, mainly in public interiors, a specially designed motif creates a whole grid, suspended as a decorative ceiling. An entire façade, on the other hand, is structured by the rhythm of the windows, especially when they are close enough to form a whole with the solid parts of the wall. An interesting example of that is the façade of the Princess Hotel near Sofia Central Railway Station. Furthermore, the flat wall is articulated by the grid of its cladding – be it brick, wood, stone, or even tiling.

Human perception is so creative that large, even, and unstructured surfaces are unable to focus our attention. On an intuitive level we need details and their garrulity. It is due to them that places are more tightly engraved in our memory and easily return to us when we try to recall them.

Details are outbursts of creative power in the most characteristic parts of the building. As previously mentioned, these are areas of transition that mark a border – for instance, between inside and outside, as is the case with doors and windows, and at the junction between wall and roof. Ornaments cover cornices and eaves and appear around edges or at the places where different materials meet. Details emphasise and complement the first two, bigger and more abstract, levels of perceiving a building; they are its own specific slang, its concrete architectural way of speaking.

Intermediate spaces and in-between areas are both parts of a building and of its surrounding space. The balconies, the window openings, and the entrances, all possess that ambiguity, as they are barriers between outside and inside on the one hand, but connections between them on the other. The dual role of such elements is the reason why they receive such special design attention.

One specific intermediate space is the staircase. Various transitions with multiple levels of meaning take place in it. At first glance, a stair represents the simple change from a common horizontal movement to a more unusual vertical one. In fact, the space of the staircase is the vertical axis inside the building which a priori grants it a special role in the entire design. The concept of transition finds yet another connotation in the stair as an intermediate zone between the public space outside the building and the completely private area of the individual apartments. So, there are two equally important reasons why the staircase of a building is a design element that necessitates special attention. It possesses, on the one hand, a radically different geometry with a high potential for a strong expressiveness. On the other hand, it is semantically loaded with possibilities for various interpretations of its intermediacy. Each part of the space and its elements is worthy of becoming the main character, starting from the steps and the landings, continuing with the ceilings, and ending with the handrails. In that company, space itself plays a very special role. Because of its verticality, its proportions, and direction, it seems rather unusual, and therefore its geometry has a very strong impact on us and could be regarded as a detail in itself.

While staircases are semi-public spaces that remain unperceivable from outside

Sofia University – St Kliment Ohridski, 15 Tsar Osvoboditel Blvd, architects of the Northern wing: Lyuben Konstantinov, 1952, Spas Rangelov, 1985

DSK Bank (former Bank of Sofia, State Savings Bank) 19 Moskovska St, architects: Georgi Fingov, Dimo Nichev, Nikola Jurukov, sculptor: Marin Vassilev, 1913

Balkan Bank, 9 Dyakon Ignatiy St, architect: Emil Hoppe, 1910

Ministry of Interior Affairs, 29 6th September St, architect: Georgi Ovcharov, 1936–1940

The Seat of the Bishop of Sofia, 6 Sveta Nedelya Sq/7 Tsar Kaloyan St, architects: Panteley Tsvetkov, 1932

Apartment building, 58 Vasil Levski Blvd, unknown architect, ca. 1940

Apartment building, 135 Georgi S. Rakovski St, unknown architect, late 1930s

National Gallery – Square 500 (former National Gallery for Foreign Arts), 1 19th February St, architects: Nikola Nikolov, Liliana Stoynova, 1987

Radevs' apartment building, 67 Hristo Botev Blvd, architect: Kostadin Mumdzhiev, 1932

Fingov's house, 38 Shipka St, architect: Georgi Fingov, 1908

Military Publishing House, 21 6th September St, architect: Georgi Ovcharov, 1943

Halite Central Covered Market, 25 Knyaginya Maria Luiza Blvd, architect: Naum Torbov, artworks: Haralambi Tachev, stone carving: Georgi Kiselinchev, 1911

Military Publishing House, 21 6th September St, architect: Georgi Ovcharov, 1943

Urban Module (UM) offices,
84 Aleksandar Stamboliyski Blvd,
architect: AEDES Studio, 2012

Apartment building, 20 Sheynovo St,
unknown architect, ca. 1940

Apartment building, 24 Ivan Vazov St,
architect: Bogdan Tomalevsk, ca. 1970s

Balabanov's house, 3 Oborishte St, architect:
Maria Berova-Haning, 1938

Trivium apartment complex, 51 Bulgaria
Blvd, Motopista District, architect:
Projects GS, 2007

Jaclyn residential building,
8 Bulgaria Blvd, architect: AEDES Studio,
2007

a building, there is another similar type of space which is private yet still publicly visible. Terraces and balconies, which, though horizontal themselves, are vertically arranged along the façade. They again act as a double bind, being part of a private inner space protruding to the outside and at the same time becoming part of the street. As balconies are places of concentrated meaning and also help to form the face of a building, the design of their parapets has always been a challenge for architects. Parapets are elements that work at various distances, and therefore need to have two different scales. One of these is linked to the way they are grasped from the street, and in that case only the eye is involved. The other scale of the parapet ensues from its relation to the inner space of the building, which turns it into a proper interior element. Thus, the parapet needs to be fine enough to be touched by hand.

The ritual is often regarded as the parade suite of life. Without that official garment, the full austerity and crudeness of life is revealed. Regarded in the light of these words, the detail could be perceived as an architectural ritual, a full-dress uniform, which, if taken away, leaves behind only the rough construction mass.

The detail is always concrete. As it is perceived from a close distance, its size is relative to the human scale, and it pops out from the general silhouette of the building. That concreteness requires a precise making, which in turn presupposes an overall positive impression of a building. For precise and skilful making means effort, real physical effort and masterly craftsmanship. In the same spirit, contemporary architectural details require the hard intellectual efforts of their invention.

The visible skills and efforts spent by others in the environment we inhabit evoke a sense of care and responsibility in us as observers. The detail is the expression of an attitude towards the inhabitants of a city and its connoisseurs. Any type of effort is intuitively grasped by our brains, even though we might not be fully aware/acquainted with the exact process of making a building and its details. The mind always seeks order; it is enchanted by it. Therefore, after we have subconsciously noted signs of human efforts aimed at one goal, we then deliberately attempt to look back and recover the whole process. And, last but not least, the qualitative efforts concentrated on a city enhance the sense of community within it.

The architectural detail in Sofia is a liberal one – it does not accept limitations in its sources of reference and thus collects new images and variations from everywhere. The layers of time through which the city has passed accumulate like molluscs upon a ship's hull and continue to tell stories of different influences, dreams, and references. That detail is a hybrid one – by definition and probably not after its own will. In each of its manifestations, it easily combines several architectural languages and blends them into a new, coherent entity. Over the years, this hybridising spirit has not only affected Sofia's local architects. Its impact has been even stronger on newcomers – individuals who arrived with their own homogeneous cultural identity and then interpreted it through the prism of local influences. One such new-comer who left a deep trace on the city was the Austrian architect Friedrich Grünanger, who dedicated much of his creative powers to the landmark buildings of National Romanticism.

A history of architectural details enables us to grasp Sofia's true character, its personality, its fingerprint, the chromosome of its genes.

After having paid so much attention to the details on buildings, let us for a moment step back and turn our gaze towards some of the sculptures and memorials in Sofia – for, in a way, they are the details of the city itself, forming part of its collective memory, and some of them long ago turned into landmarks.

As the lion has a very special place in the Bulgarian national consciousness, a 'lion line' could be traced in the centre of

Sofia, starting from Lions' Bridge (198), running through the Courthouse (016), and ending in South Park, in front of the National Palace of Culture (167, 140). The four sculptures on Lions' Bridge commemorate the four booksellers sentenced to death and hung on the site. Two immense lions guard the entrance to the Courthouse. Approaching from Lions' Bridge, the first one, the one to the north, seems to be quite an ordinary lion. The second one, however, has received a nickname which translates as something like the 'Perplexed Lion' because of the unnatural position of its paws. Because of its strangeness and its central place in the city, the Perplexed Lion has become a common meeting spot for people, even in the era of mobile phones.

The last location on the lion line is quite new to Sofia, as it replaced a monument that was erected along with the National Palace of Culture to mark the 1,300th anniversary of the Bulgarian State. The 1,300 Years of Bulgaria monument, which was demolished in 2017, was the subject of passionate debate. It was associated with the communist regime and was much hated for its brutalist aesthetic. However, others liked it precisely because of its brutalist aesthetic. The new, replacement monument is an attempt to continue the tradition of lions on memorials. In fact, the lion was taken from a previous monument which existed on the site before the erection of the National Palace of Culture, but it now seems rather inappropriate in relation to the surrounding cityscape. As the new monument involves the restoration of military memorial, it leads to another reference: the Monument to the Unknown Soldier, which includes a sculpture of a lion that guards the eternal flame on the southern side of St Sofia Church (061).

St Alexander Nevski Cathedral: detail of throne designed by Alexander Jakovlev

Now, after having altered the focus of the eyepiece through which we've been observing Sofia in detail, and then changing our focus again, in order to have a look at some of Sofia's characteristic monuments, let us now once more turn to the urban scale depicted on our tourist maps. From there, three types of structure are clearly discernible: the fine grainy surface of the houses in the villages adjoining the city; moving inwards, to a circle of residential complexes from the 1970s onwards, which have a much larger, simpler geometry; and finally, inwards again, enclosed in that irregular ring is the city centre with its classical urban structure, outlining the firm grid of the streets and the pulsating spaces of the inner courts.

In that final inner part of the city, two areas stand out from the surrounding urban fabric. The first is the National Palace of Culture (140), with its park piercing the city from the south. The Vitosha Boulevard to the north connects the palace to the second area: the Largo complex (019) of three State buildings. Though the western axis is clearly delineated, its eastern extension more interesting. For, if we follow it from its beginning at the Largo, we notice a pulsating zigzag of alternating green areas and street facades along Tzar Osvoboditel Boulevard. Towards the east the fluctuating area widens, as it also includes the space around St Alexander Nevski Cathedral, and gradually increases in scale, coming to an end at the Eagles' Bridge, where the Knyajeska Garden merges into Boris's Garden.

From our bird's-eye view, this chain of larger public buildings and the open spaces between them is clearly discernible from the fabric of the surrounding residential areas. Thus, on the scale of our tourist maps, the details of the city turn out to be not the smallest but the largest – and maybe the most important – of its elements.

CONAP apartment building, 73 Bulgaria Blvd, Manastirski Livadi District, architects: Projects GS

CONAP apartment building, 73 Bulgaria Blvd, Manastirski Livadi District, architects: Projects GS

St Paraskeva Church, 58 Georgi S. Rakovski St, architect: Anton Torniov, 1930, iconostasis: Todor Hristov, Ivan Travnitski, 1940

Apartment building, 149 Georgi S. Rakovski St, architect: Hristo Berberov, 1937

Public Mineral Baths, 1 Banski Sq, architect: Emil von Foerster, 1893, plastic elements, ceramics, and decoration: Haralampi Tachev, Stefan Dimitrov, 1904

Theodora and Stefan Peykov's apartment building, 10 Tsar Osvoboditel Blvd, architect: Vasko Vassilev, 1939

Angel Kantardzhiev's house, Tsar Osvoboditel Blvd, architects: Ivan Vasilyov and Dimitar Tsolov, project: 1932

Angel Kantardzhiev's house, Tsar Osvoboditel Blvd, architects: Ivan Vasilyov and Dimitar Tsolov, project: 1932

Apartment building, Osogovo St, unknown architect, 1932

Workers' Hospital (today Queen Giovanna Hospital), 8 Byalo More St, architect: Georgi Ovcharov, project: 1927, built: 1930–1935

Research Institute at the Faculty of Agronomy (today Sofia District Court and Prosecution), architect: Georgi Ovcharov, 1936

Buyuk Mosque/UL Mosque/Grand Vizier Mahmud Pasha Mosque (today National Archaeological Institute and Museum), 1 Knyaz Alexander I Battenberg Sq

Workers' Hospital (today Queen Giovanna Hospital), 8 Byalo More St, architect: Georgi Ovcharov, project: 1927, built: 1930–1935

Lyubata apartment building, 12 Lyubata St, architects: AEDES studio, 2012

National Health Institute, 26 Yanko Sakuzov Blvd, architects: Todor Zlatev and Dimitar Koev, 1932

POPO single family residence, 'Henri van de Velde door', Simeonovo District, architects: Projects GS, 2000

America for Bulgaria Foundation, previously Andrey Arsov's family house, 6 Malyovitsa St, architect: Karl Heinrich; facade decoration: Andreas Greis, 1910

Apartment building, 28 Patriarch Evtimiy Blvd, architect: Vasko Vassilev, 1935

Rayna Pudareva's building, 1 Tsar Samuil St, architect: Kostadin Mumdzhiev, 1934

St Paraskeva Church, 58 Georgi Sava Rakovski St, architect: Anton Torniov, 1930, iconostasis: Todor Hristov, Ivan Travnitski, 1940

German School, today Music Academy, 94 Evlogi and Hristo Georgievi Blvd, 1934

Hotel complex and Bulgaria Concert Hall, 4 Tsar Osvoboditel Blvd, architects: Stancho Belkovski and Ivan Danchov, 1934–1937

Bulgarian National Bank, 1 Knyaz Alexander I Battenberg Sq, architects: Ivan Vasilyov, Dimitar Tsolov, B. Kapitanov, 1934–1939

Red Apple apartment building, 24 Byala Cherkva St, architects: AEDES Studio, 2012

Red Apple apartment building, 24 Byala Cherkva St, architects: AEDES Studio, 2012

Red Apple Apartments, 24 Byala Cherkva St, architects: AEDES Studio, 2012

Red Apple Apartments, 24 Byala Cherkva St, architects: AEDES Studio, 2012

Faculty of Agronomy, architects: Georgi Ovcharov and Genko Popov, 1924–1930

Angel Kantardzhiev's house, Tzar Osvoboditel Blvd, architects: Ivan Vasilyov and Dimitar Tsolov, project: 1932

Remains of an Ottoman religious object (mihrab wall), 1 Stara Stena St, 16th century

Red Apple apartment building, 24 Byala Cherkva St, architect: AEDES Studio, 2012

Angel Kantardzhiev's house, Tsar Osvoboditel Blvd, architects: Ivan Vasilyov and Dimitar Tsolov, project: 1932

Rayna Pudareva's building, 1 Tsar Samuil St, architect: Kostadin Mumdzhiev, 1934

Boyana Inclined Apartments, 14 Botko Voyvoda St, 2010

Angel Kantardzhiev's house, Tsar Osvoboditel Blvd, architects: Ivan Vasilyov and Dimitar Tsolov, project: 1932

Cooperative apartment building, 27 William Gladstone St, architect: Vasko Vassilev, 1943

Apartment building, 55 Exarch Joseph St, unknown architect, ca. 1934